Personal Journal For Yesterday, Now, and Tomorrow

and Other Selected Poems

S. Gordden Link
(1907 - 1986)

Personal Journal For Yesterday, Now, and Tomorrow
and Other Selected Poems

S. Gordden Link

edited with an introduction by

Bruce Souders
Professor Emeritus
Shenandoah University

Published at
Shenandoah University
Winchester, Virginia 22601
1992

We gratefully acknowledge the following sources of the poetry published in this volume: Library of Congress Permanent Collection of Modern Poetry (Recorded 1961 and 1973); *The Saturday Review of Literature; The Christian Century; Poetry: A Magazine of Verse; The Golden Book; Potomac Magazine of The Washington Post; Andover Review; Miscellany; Poetry World; Versecraft; Plain Talk; Unity; The Reach of Song; Poetry Review; Choir Practice; The Peabody Reflector and Alumni News; American Poetry; The Campus Scope* of Anne Arundel County Community College; *Bozart; Contemporary Verse; The Crossroads Magazine; The New York Times; Contemporary Vision; Rebel Poet; The Westminster Magazine; Three Poems for Now;* publications of prize-winning poems of The Poetry Society of America; *Christ in the Breadline; Reveille: Anthology of Poems by Members of the Armed Forces; The Diamond Anthology* and *The Golden Year Anthology* of the Poetry Society of America; *The Golden Anniversary Anthology* of the Poetry Society of Viriginia; and *Grub Street Book of Verse*.

Copyright © Bruce Souders 1992

ISBN No.: 0-9634744-0-5

All rights reserved. No part of this book may be reproduced or transmitted in any form or by any means electronic or mechanical, including photocopying, recording, or any information storage and retrieval system without written permission of the editor.

TABLE OF CONTENTS

INTRODUCTION ix
Christ in the Breadline and Other Early Poems 1
   In Beauty Now 3
   The Dead Have Peace 3
   Let There Be Rain 4
   Professor Pendleton's Garden 5
   Ultimate Limit 5
   The Tenement..6
   God Did Not Make Cities 8
   Soliloquy in a Sweatshop 9
   To Those Who Have No Work 9
   Prairie Pilgrimage 10
   Complaint 10
   Mountain Man Now 11
   Scrap Metal in the Collection Plate 12
   Munich 12
   Christ in the Breadline (Selections) 13
      The Prodigal Christ 13
      Prodigal Son 13
      The Mulatto Addresses His Savior on Christmas Day ..13
      Roman Carpenter on a Good Friday 14
      I Dreamed I Was the Lord 15
      Peter...15
      Mass Crucifixion 16

Selected Poems 1934 - 1974...19
   I. Personal Journal 19
      The Deaf (For My Father) 21
      Artist and Ape...22
      Grammarian's Grave 23
      Capillary Signpost...24
      The Leader..25
      The Color of Danger..26
      The Golden Eagle 30
      Minor Variations on the Theme of Dogwoods........30
         i. Accident 30

        ii. Struggle 31
        Professor's Office 32
        My Hereafter 33
        In Memoriam (For F.D.R.) 35
        Silver Lady 36

   II. The Strange Noise of Freedom 37
        The Strange Noise of Freedom 39
        Land He Fought For 44

   III. People..47
        Anonymous Obit 49
        Services for the Dead: A Minor Greek Tragedy 49
        My Failing Student 50
        Lecture by a Visiting Poet.....................................50
        e. e. 51
        A Memory of Dark Hair 52
        Old Men..52
        English Professor 53
        Kansan Poet Far From Home 54

   IV. Places...55
        A Pause in Arlington Cementery 57
        The Round Rocks of Palestine 59
        Hospitals..60
        Dubious Conquest 60
        Letter from Cairo (Selection) 62
        Veteran's Hospital 65
        Reunion in Foxhole 65

   V. Things 67
        Answer to the Critics of a Poet (For Jesse Stuart) .69
        Frustration 69
        Rondeau to Suppressed Ego 69
        Staging Area Concerto (Selections) 70
            The Telephone Booth 70
            T V 71
            The Picture 72

VI. The Edge of Oblivion 73
    Poetry and Physics 75
    The Little People 76
    Apocalypse 79
    Ultimate Weapon 80
    The Edge of Oblivion 82
        i. Final Curtain 82
        ii. Now at the Edge of Oblivion: Memories of
            Harvard at Midcentury 84
        iii. The Last Stand 86
    And Now in Search of Peace 87

VII. *The Tired Heart: A Cardiac Biography* 89
    Noise of Futility 91
    Noblesse Oblige 91
    Would the Heart Escape 92
    "In the Heart's Deep Care" 92
    Spring and the Tired Heart 93
    Strange Odyssey...93
    "Dead"..94

VIII. The Last Day 95
    On Being Thirteen in 1970 97
    Shelter From Oblivion 98
    Martial Concert for a Dubious Place 100
    The Last Day 101
    The Last Burlesque Show 104
    Singing Mother 104
    Concrete Rhapsody in Georgia 105
    A Prayer for John McEnroe Before Wimbledon ..106
    Prayer for a Second Planting 106
    A Balladelle of Foxhunting 108
    The Singing Men 109
    Esoteric Question 110

INTRODUCTION

At the age of seventeen, Gordden Link (Seymour Gordden Link, Seymour G. Link, S. Gordden Link) became a member of the Poetry Society of America upon nomination of Harriet Monroe, Editor of *Poetry: A Magazine of Verse*, and Corinne Roosevelt Robinson, both of whom saw a great future for him as a poet. He remained a member of the Society until his death June 21, 1986, to establish the longest continuous membership in its history. During that period, he participated in its political battles, won some of its poetry contests, and judged even more of them.

However, at his death, he was still looking for the elusive combination of poems that would interest a publisher and justify the faith of his sponsors to PSA membership. Much of what he repeatedly tried to forge into a viable collection was by the time of his last attempts in the early 1980s more than thirty years old. Furthermore, the torrents of individually published poems that characterized his earlier years (about 400 published poems by 1960) had slowed to a trickle. Nevertheless, even in these later years, countless people called him "poet" and considered him their mentor: high school students in Warren Country, Virginia; students at Shenandoah University, Winchester, Virginia, where he had served as Writer-in-Residence between 1970 and 1983; those who had sat under his tutelage in writers' conferences from Maryland to Georgia; and others who had sent him work for criticism or publication in anthologies he was always projecting but never completing.

Seymour Gordden Link was born in Chicago, Illinois, April 9, 1907, to Joseph and Florence Tannenholz Link. An only child, he received encouragement and the undivided attention of his parents. While his father looked after the physical needs of his family as an upholsterer and manufacturer of quality furniture for the wealthy and socially prominent, his mother provided Seymour with the best education the family could afford. During the Chicago years and later during the early New York Years, this meant governesses and tutors when she herself was involved in cultural activities outside the home. Early on, she nurtured her son's love of the arts by providing instruction in painting, the violin, and poetry writing. It was in the latter endeavor that she gave him strongest encouragement. At one point shortly before her death, she even attended a course in poetry writing with him at New York

University. The strong bond between Gordden and his mother haunted him all his life.(Cf. "A Memory of Dark Hair," p. 52.)

Link's high school years at Erasmus High School in New York City seemed to follow the pattern of those of other young men of the time: part time jobs, athletic competition (boxing and wrestling were his specialities), flirtation with a number of career possibilities (medicine, writing, teaching, professional boxing, detective work), extra-curricular activities (mostly of a literary sort), and of course, his academic work, which seemed all too easy for him because of the cultural environment of his home

Wanting desperately to be a poet, he typed and hand-bound, with fabric from his father's upholstery shop, two volumes of poetry: *Subways and Prairie Dogs* (1928, almost six years after Harriet Monroe had published "The Mulatto" in *Poetry: A Magazine of Verse*) and *Poets Should Never Die* (1927). These still remain among his papers at Shenandoah University

After he had enrolled at NYU, he met Carl Sandburg when the city editor of the Brooklyn *Standard-Union* assigned him to cover the poet's reading-recital. Almost four decades later, he described the experience in the "Forward" to Hazel Durnell's *The America of Carl Sandburg*:

> Having raised a mustache for this job [as a cub reporter] and having carefully cultivated the upturned brim of battered felt hat and the generally cynical posture of the era's city room, I nevertheless gave way to frenetic excitement of my first meeting with the man whose poetry I had been aping for some two years. . .

Exhilarated by this experience, he wrote a term paper for a sophomore English course under what he himself called a "pretentious" title: "Carl Sandburg's Philosophy of Life." In 1930, a revision of this paper was published in the British journal, *Poetry Review* (Vol. XXI, 1930, p. 423). According to Ms. Durnell, this was the "first analysis of Sandburg's philosophy to appear in a British journal."

Link's meeting with Sandburg resulted in a short-lived correspondence between the two men; but it was on the wane when they got together again in Nashville, Tennessee, about six years later. Link was enrolled as a graduate student at George Peabody College of Teachers, now a part of Vanderbilt University. Sandburg had come to town to give a reading. Link and a friend,

Ralph Wickeiser, secreted Sandburg into their quarters in the dormitory. They stayed up almost all night discussing the "New Poetry" and singing to guitar accompaniment by both Sandburg and Link. Later, Dean Ida Z. Carr admonished Link for creating a disturbance; he tried to explain that he had been entertaining Carl Sandburg. She replied, "Kindly do me the favor of not adding prevarication to your other shortcomings." There appears to be no official record of this "misdemeanor," but it is recalled in later years in correspondence from friends of Link in Nashville.

Link gives Sandburg credit for nudging him into paying closer attention to Mae Mills, president of Peabody Poets and, according to Sandburg, "the prettiest little Southern girl I have seen on this trip." Link and Mills were married January 11, 1936. About three years later, when the Links were teaching at St. Lawrence University, Gordden started one of his first of several collections of poetry centered around "The Strange Noise of Freedom," which was published as a single poem in *The Saturday Review of Literature*, March 10, 1945. In the projected collection of his own poetry in 1939, Link wrote of "The Strange Noise of Freedom."

> This poem is dedicated to Carl Sandburg from whom I received my earliest poetic stimulation and to whom I have long been indebted for a richness of living about which only he and one other have knowledge; and the book to which it will give name will also carry the same dedication.

There were other influences in the poetic development of Gordden Link. One was his association with The Rebel Poets, Internationale of Song, headed by Ralph Cheney. The editor of its official organ, *Rebel Poets*, was Jack Conroy, author of *The Disinherited*, an influential though not widely circulated "proletarian novel" until its revival a few years after it was first published. Among others associated with or published by the Rebel Poets were Lucia Trent, Norman MacLeod, Kenneth Porter, Carl Sandburg, and Louis Ginsburg, father of Allen Ginsburg. Link's affiliation with the group antedated his going to Nashville and coincided with his graduate and postgraduate studies along the Eastern Seaboard: NYU (MA, 1930), Harvard (MEd, 1932), Yale, and Columbia. It opened avenues for publication of his own poetry in the organization's house organs (*The Rebel Poets* and annual anthologies titled *Unrest*) and like minded journals in England, translation, and editorial work with The Driftwind Press in Vermont. He and Kenneth Porter edited several chapbooks for Driftwind. It was also Driftwind that published *Christ in the Breadline*, an anthology of poems for Christmas and Lent by Link, Porter, and Harry Elmore Hurd, a former U.S. Army Chaplain.

In later years, Link tried to disassociate himself from what Rebel Poets professed in their "Manifesto," published in January 1931: "Art for Humanity's Sake" and criticism of perceived inhumanities in American life. In language with Marxist overtones, it had advocated war against "imperialism" and capitalism and had espoused a "cooperative society." Much of its poetry had been strident and deliberately controversial.

In New England, Link made a literary connection outside Rebel Poets that was more lasting. It was Rollo Walter Brown of Harvard. Not only did Brown and Link keep up a lively correspondence for years. They shared the joys of one another's successes and the heartaches of their failures. Frequently, Link found himself a promoter for Brown's lectures.

In 1934, Link left Boston, returned to Limestone College, where he had been teaching for a year prior to taking up graduate work again. However, he was soon on his way to George Peabody College, where he had received a teaching fellowship. These were the Depression years and one had to be practical. There was no money in organizing poetry clubs and editing magazines like *Poetry World*. Neither was there security in education unless one had advanced degrees. Nevertheless, Link had misgivings about taking a PhD degree because of what it might do to his interest in writing poetry, not to mention his success as a poet. His friends Cheney and Trent, who were really husband and wife, had frequently addressed the problem. Here is an excerpt from a letter they wrote in 1932:

> We don't think you should feel one bit discouraged about your poetic progress. Of course, to be a PhD and a poet is almost impossible and next to unprecedented, but you'll achieve the miracle with colors flying. The other night we visited the fellow who was the best poet in my college class, when my work was punk, and found that he was shrivelled into a dry, brittle stalk rattling meaninglessly in the stale air of the college halls where he is now a mediocre professor. But you're not made of stuff like that. In all honesty, your work seems to us to have deepened its roots and lifted its branches

and flowered with fragrance and beauty drenching the air. I constantly feel that my best work is behind me and then write something I feel is better than what I've done before, little as that may be.

At Peabody, Link became involved in poetry again as a lecturer in the extension division and founder of, and advisor to, Peabody Poets. He also took advantage of every opportunity to move in the literary circles across the way at Vanderbilt University. Though not as intimate as those he had made in New England, Link's contacts included the Rhodes Scholar, critic, teacher, poet and prime mover of the Fugitives, John Crowe Ransom, and Donald Davidson. Here is how Dr. Mae Mills Link assesses the transformation of her late husband after coming to Nashville:

> Gordden became a split personality in the period leading up to World War II - he could not abandon the "loud" poets, but as he understood the quiet Vanderbilt group and others such as T. S. Eliot, he was drawn into the heritage of John Donne, Gerard Manley Hopkins, and a whole new world. This was, in part, because in the 1936-37 academic year, I was working on my master's degree under John Crowe Ransom and entertained the dream of writing the definitive work on T. S. Eliot. However, Ransom in his courtly, Old South manner firmly insisted it was time to write about Edna St. Vincent Millay. Only a woman could do it, and I was one of two women students being guided through graduate study by him at that time. Gordden, meanwhile, was writing what were nothing more than finger exercises as he continued toward the doctorate and the completion of his dissertation. I had to push hard to get him to complete his PhD in 1938.

Gordden Link found more to do in Nashville than marriage, graduate studies, and finger exercises in poetry. He became involved in WPA projects that included writing a play and editing the *Tennessee State Guide* (1936-38); and he associated with the McKendree Methodist Church and its pastor King Vivien. Link had been converted to Methodism under the Methodist Episcopal Church North; but here in Nashville, he was working in the Methodist Episcopal Church South. It is not clear whether he had been officially named director of youth activities, or perhaps even assistant minister, but he was deeply enough involved in the life of the congregation to catch the excitement that existed over the prospects that by mid-1939 all branches of American Methodism would be united, healing wounds that had festered since before the Civil War. When the merger sessions were held in Nashville, Link served as a volunteer with King Vivien, one of the secretaries for the meeting. His affiliation with Methodism and its orientation toward the Social Gospel offered Link an opportunity to practice the concern for humanity he had been expressing in his earlier poetry and his association with Rebel Poets, some of whom had been Christian social activists.

The academic year 1938-39 found the Links at Oglethorpe University as members of the English Department. In addition, Gordden performed some of the functions of chaplain and served as consultant to the Oglethorpe University Press and Managing Editor of *The Westminster Magazine*. Mae was Fiction Editor of the latter. During the summer of 1939, Gordden went to St. Lawrence University as a visiting professor; and that fall both Links joined the faculty there, he as Assistant Professor in English and Civilization and she as an instructor in the English Department. After another summer at St. Lawrence, they moved to Drury College in Missouri for the 1940-41 academic year, he as head of the English Department and she as an instructor.

As it became more apparent that the United States would become involved in World War II, the Links returned to Georgia, making their home at Warm Springs, where Mae was employed by the Warm Springs Foundation as Director of Education while Gordden began his military career. It started with his appointment as a major in the Georgia State Guard, after which he became Director of Training and Personnel at Microstat Corporation in New England. There he prepared training manuals, organized training centers from Connecticut to California, and served as a consultant in military microfilming and representative in the Training Within Industry Group of the War Production Board.

In 1942 he entered full time military service with an appointment to the Army Specialist Corps. Subsequently he was assigned to duties as a coordinator of enemy films and related educational, editorial, and intelligence functions. Tours of duty took him to North Africa twice, to the British Isles, and to the Middle East. He was present at Cairo in 1943 and Yalta in 1945, where he served as a courier. In 1946, he was recalled to the Pentagon to be an editor with the War Department Special Staff Historical Division.

After his discharge in 1947, he continued as a civilian employee with the Army Department of History. Until May 7, 1948, he was Chief Historian and Editorial Director of General MacArthur's Engineers Historical Project in Baltimore, Maryland. This location gave him an opportunity to return to academic life at The Johns Hopkins University. There he founded the writing workshop at McCoy College and organized the Hilltop Writers Conference in connection with Hilltop Theatre. As time permitted, but often on a full time basis, he served a number of other academic institutions in the Washington-Baltimore area while continuing editorial and educational assignments for the Army, both as a civilian and as a reserve officer. Among them were Anne Arundel Community College in Severna Park, Maryland; Loyola College, Baltimore; Dumbarton College of Holy Cross Institute for Adult Education, Washington; and Southeastern University. In every instance, he concentrated on helping young writers and conducting workshops to which he invited his literary associates to read their works and lecture.

Meanwhile, Link was engaging in numerous other activities that often diluted his effectiveness in any one of them. He became a book reviewer for *The Saturday Review of Literature*, which had been publishing his poetry even while he was overseas. He served as director of the King-Smith School of Creative Arts during its closing months, hoping to revive it according to its original premises - "that life and the Arts are inseparable, that preparation for expression in art must in the largest sense be preparation for living, [and] that the artist has a definite and significant place in a society that finds itself entering upon a new era." (The King-Smith School had been founded in 1925 and closed in 1948.) He became affiliated with, and subsequently directed entirely, The University Press of Washington. This press had, for a time, close ties to The Library of Congress, where Link became familiar with not only the Librarians but also their Consultants in Poetry. This connection led to his reading for the permanent collection of recordings featuring contemporary poets reading their own works. Finally, for about thirteen years, he conducted Link Associates, Consulting Psychologists, and helped organize the short lived American Association for Social Psychiatry.

This welter of activity gave a semblance of fulfilled prophecy to "Complaint" (p. 10) and "Frustration," a poem Link wrote at the age of 23 and revised later (p. 69). He provided life a battle ground for struggles that sapped his creative energies and badgered his sense of place and purpose.

The last two decades were painful for Gordden Link. Though he had become a wiser man in the ways of the world during his years in the military, he had not learned how to harness his dreams - how to be practical. He could not let go of the past and he did not understand the present. That is why he spent so much time trying to revise his early poems for publication. He was hounded by ill health and occasional bouts of depression, often lacking the resilience to roll with the punches of life. He felt passed by as a poet and rejected by the very people he wanted so desperately to help. When younger generations treated him with benign neglect or accused him of name-dropping as he spoke of writers he had known, he forged what had been a gentle irony in much of his early poetry with a social theme into a devastating, rusty sword and slashed his critics. He was driven by obsessions. One was the fear of growing old, an obsession aggravated by guilt over impatience with his aging father (Cf. "Old Men," p. 52). Another was the potential for destroying the human race through nuclear war. The root of this fear was his reconnaissance flight to photograph the results of atomic blasts at Hiroshima; and yet, much as he feared nuclear war, he was uncomfortable, even angry, in the presence of war protesters.

Link's association with Shenandoah University began when he and Mrs. Link bought Dellbrook, in Riverton, Virginia. They had dreams of turning it into a retreat for writers - especially poets and scholars; but episodes of ill health for both of them crippled the enterprise from the outset. From 1970 to 1982, Gordden served Shenandoah as Writer-in-Residence, and from 1969 to 1983, as Director of the Dellbrook-Shenandoah College and Conservatory Writers Conference.

* * *

It is now time to acknowledge people to whom I am indebted in bringing out this volume. Dr. Mae Link deserves my deepest appreciation for her patience during the long hours we spent sorting papers, rereading individual poems, and taping conversations. Ilse Jenkins has given us days of typing material available only in brittle, faded manuscripts; and Dr. Joanne Jacobs has assisted in many ways from proofreading to helping select some of the poems. Gordden's friends of former years have given me insight into his life and work that had remained hidden from me during the years he and I worked together at Shenandoah University. Malinda Feathers has patiently and professionally done the word processing in preparing the final manuscript. My wife, Pat, has had to cope with the temporal and spatial indignities I heaped upon her sense of order around the house from time to time. As a friend observed, "There should be a special novena for what she puts up with." Finally, I join Dr. Mae Link in acknowledging the encouragement and support of Dr. James A. Davis, President of Shenandoah University, where Dr. Gordden Link's papers are now housed.

                                            April 15, 1992
                                            Bruce Souders
                                            Literary Executer, Link papers
                                            Professor Emeritus
                                            Shenandoah University

Christ in the Breadline
and Other Early Poems

In Beauty Now

In beauty now there is a sharper pain;
There is a deeper hurt in purple skies.
I cannot see a cloud or watch suns rise
But cry that you will never know again
These things. Or silver sparrows in the rain
And shining summer sidewalks as the rain dries,
Or the glory of our garden and the young bird cries,
The spring odor of the grasses where the snow has lain.

I ache that you have left these things behind;
The beauty that we shared I have alone.
You never should have left it all to me,
You quiet singer who must now be blind
To everything that we have always known
Oh, seeing now, I would I could not see!

The Dead Have Peace

Only the dead have peace, only the dead
Who have no earthly need to wake from sleep;
With earth below and earth above the head,
They have no earthly need, no need to weep.
But we who have earth beneath our feet
Must look ahead to restless, sorry years.
There is no turning on our dusty street
And we have time, yes, too much time, for tears.

Only the dead knows peace, for he, alone,
May have a certain guarantee of rest
Who bears six feet of earth and carven stone
Upon the placid marble of his breast,
Who, having left all earthly things behind,
Beneath the earth, is comfortably blind.

Let There Be Rain

Lord, let the rain come down.

Let the rain come down and wash the faces
of the guant gray towers
that yearn for a touch of the sky.

Let the rain come down,
quick and cool, and fast as the flight
of silver dreams before the light of day

To make a million little geysers leap
from the dark road,
from the black wet walk.

Let the rain come down
to cool the day that has burned to a crisp
in the steady flame of long desire.

Let the quiet, cooling quicksilver slide
upon my burning brow,
caress my glowing cheeks,

For a moment quench the fire
that is raging in my brain.
Lord, let there be rain.

Let the rain come down
and the wet breeze laugh
as the happy waters dance on their way
to earthly water carnival.

Let the rustling russet leaves
sing their swan songs to the trees
as each sheet of silver laughter
spills against their shrunken breasts.

Let the sudden soothing wetness drench
man and beast and beaten bird
and joust against the eager earth,
a leaping multi-faceted illusion.

Let the rain come prancing
in quiet throbbing ecstacy
of quickening delight;
a thousand places delved at once
by living water, myriad clowns.

Lord, let the rain come down.

Professor Pendleton's Garden

This is the classroom God intended. Trees
For cloistered walls, and slabs of rock for seats,
And earnest pilgrims, elbows fast to knees,
Leaning toward the fire, letting the heat's
Quick friendliness sculp beauty on their faces.
Here is a college reaching through the dark
Higher then man may build; the velvet spaces
Above our soft communion leave a mark
Upon our hearts no lifting chapel might.

A school's not bigger than the space it gives
The mind to grow in; we have all the night
Drawing us out and up, and each one lives
A richer hour . . . the way, it well may be,
They did at secret fires in Galilee.

Ultimate Limit

A bottle marked a quart will hold a quart
or maybe less, but surely never more;
and any blood will spurt like any port
when its container holds more than its store.

My blood has stretched its walls these many
                                           months
like wine that has fermented overlong;
once it was not this way; I wandered once
cool. And my heart was calm, and cool my song.
My body was designed for so much torque
and no erg more. But malice, hate, and scorn
bittered the quiet dregs. And now the cork
is burst of pressures never to be borne.

Pluck you your skirts away or rubric fjord
will stain them . . . much as if by shot or
                                           sword!

The Tenement

All, from the tenement,
Sad-eyed and thick-tongued, went,
Hungry and cold, they went
Down to pick coal;
Coal from the railroad tracks,
Coal hugged in burlap sacks;
Sacks clutched in hungry hands
Black from the coal.

Weary and wan, they went,
Trudging with bodies bent,
Bent from the burlap sacks,
Bent from the cold.
Bending and picking crumbs,
Crumbs with hands made of thumbs;
Thumbs from anxiety and
Thumbs from the cold.

Slowly the sacks were filled,

Filled while the babes' cries shrilled,
Shrilled to the skies with their
Hunger and cold.

Slowly the trudging troop,
Bent from their steady stoop,
Turned towards the tenement,
Having grown old.

Bleeding from frozen lips,
Bleeding from finger tips;
Finger tips blackened and
Cut to the quick
Back to the tenement,
Back all the sad ones went,
Back to bear healing heat
Home to their sick.

Back, at a stumbling pace,
Cold, blued upon each face,
Sons of a sad-eyed race,
Thick-tongued they went.

* * *

Stoves were now thawing out;
Chilled ones were grouped about.
Hungry, but warm, they were
Near to content.

Slowly the fires died;
Softly the children cried;
Cried through the night for there
Was no more coal.
All, from the tenement,
Sad-eyed and thick-tongued, went,
Hungry and cold they went
Down to pick coal.

God Did Not Make the Cities

God did not make the city.
He made the wide spread field, the sheltering wood,
He made great space in his large pity
For all of Nature's brood.

He gave his creatures room,
Unbound, to move.
He did not seal their doom
Within a groove.
Masochistic man
All stifling cities built.
He made of Nature's plan
A crazy quilt.

Man burrowed under ground,
In cliffs he bored his way.
He clustered in herds, he cramped his limbs,
                          he bound
His sons to tie themselves to dark inevitable
                                   dismay.

He wrapped about his subtle chains
That hold him lonely in a crowd;
Man suffers the City's growing pains
From swaddling clothes to shroud.

To Deity man raised great towers,
In fine fanatical illusion.
His mass production, multiplying powers
Have brought him boundless Babel, have given
                                 him confusion.

Pray God that Man-Made Cities join
The ruins of Greece, the Catacombs of Rome,
That life may stride with free ungirded loin,
That man may make a home.

Soliloquy in a Sweatshop

It's good to see a strip o' sky
Show through the smoke an' grime an' dust.
It's good to heave a little sigh
When you sort o' feel you must.

It's good to have some space between
That roof-top there, and ours—
Some place that looks a little clean
And makes you think o' flowers.
To see it helps us bear our task;
It makes the slums and country kin.
O God, it isn't much we ask—
Don't let the roof-tops close us in.

To Those Who Have No Work

Nothing has more of helpless numbing terror
To those who have no work, than watching night
Black out again the shopworn hope, the "might-be,"
The tired "if" of morning. Faith is a mirror
That puts a silver edge of purposed error
Around the inward-looking one and brightly
Alters the marginal of fact. But sight
Adjusts with time, and death knells reach a hearer.

Mornings come loud, and noons are colored noise,
But then the Juggernaut of night awakens
And gathers quiet brooding force, the poise

Of even hardy unemployed is shaken.
Soon there is only this to stretch the gaze:
The slowly piling one by one of days.

Prairie Pilgrimage
(Inspired by the poetry of Kenneth W. Porter)

Though we were iron hard and wary
We felt it in the glistening air,
It followed us across the prairie. . . .
Jesus Christ was everywhere.

The prairie dogs had bleeding feet,
Pierced was each coyote's sharp-ribbed side,
And if we passed a sheaf of wheat
We saw that it was crucified.

We paused to rest at an acrid well,
Lit by a hard unwinking star,
And neither one of us could tell
If we did not drink vinegar!

Soon we saw on the horizon
The outposts of a Kansas town,
Each wired pole we set our eyes on
Darkly bore a thorned crown.

The jobless touched the town with blight,
Though some folk flaunted gold and furs;
These starved Jews, Gentiles, black and white,
We saw that they were Carpenters!

Complaint

God gave me fingers made for reaching,
Then placed me where all things are near.

He gave me tongue made for beseeching,
Then put me on a deafened sphere.

He gave me eyes designed for weeping,
Then left me where no tears are shed.
He gave me dream-thick lids for sleeping
Where sleep is only for the dead.

He gave me tears to shed for the blind
Who could not see what I was after.
He gave me goal impossible to find
And then He did not give me laughter!

Mountain Man Now
(Acrostic Sonnet to Harry Elmore Hurd, S.T.B.)

He blots out hills, he looms against the skies,
And, moving, makes the landscape sense a lack.
Rain has washed the cities from his eyes,
Raging winds have blown the mountains back.

Yosemite has molded on his face
Her granite distances. His days belong
Under the brassy suns where ranging space
Reveal to him her silence and her song.

Dawn is the only worship he has known
Since he left our candle-lighting land.
The vast stretches claim his as their own
Binding us as kin who shake his hand.

So let us follow him where mountains burn,
Leaving behind all hope for his return!

Scrap Metal in the Collection Plate
(A Christmas Poem)

No fire ever burned for very long
That had no fuel to feed its hungry tongues;
No nation ever battled with a song
Or with the wind that whistled through the lungs
Of orators. Before we cry our woe
That "heathen" troops who spurn our gentle cries
Relish their muskets better, slay their foe,
Perhaps we best had turn our bitter eyes
Upon our Christian stewards here and now
Whose noble tithe mounts so impressive high
Because the tiller beats his idle plow
To swords on which our heathen brothers die.
If thirty silver pieces fill our tray,
Recall three hundred men who fall today!

Munich

Now that the lock is broken
On the silver cage of speech,
Now that our hate is spoken
And the bird is out of reach,

What is the use of locking
The empty cage, confess!
The bird will still be mocking
Our silver quietness.
The space between the stars
Will no more let their singing
Be girded in by bars.
And hate that has been uttered
By the angry mouths of men
Will be mute when slices buttered
Become whole bread again!

CHRIST IN THE BREADLINE (Selections)

The Prodigal Christ

Strip the heavy vine
And the swollen wheat, they said.
Hold service with the rich red wine
And the small white bread.

But fatted meat we ate
That well, we knew, sufficed
Three wiser men to celebrate
The Prodigal Christ!

Prodigal Son

It was foretold . . . and Christ returned to earth!
One cold December morning in a manger
He was found by three wise men, each one a stranger
To faith, who would have shut their eyes in mirth
Had anyone suggested virgin birth
As explanation of this sudden danger
To the town's stability. The Banker, Granger,
Sheriff . . . sadly spoke about the dearth.

Jesus fled the county home. He tried
Telling men the things they had forgot
Of love and peace . . . but heedless millions died
On the silver alters of Iscariot.
The deeds of Judas blared in every headline,
But Jesus froze to death behind a breadline!

The Mulatto Addresses his Savior on Christmas Morning

Because my mother thought
That a black sin

Was white if it was brought
In a white skin,

Because my father bought
At cost of pride
The lusthead that he sought
From a black bride,

The gods bestow on me
A life of hate
The white man's gift to see
A nigger's fate.

My Lord, why have I sight
To see my lack—
Dreams of a bitter white
And soul of black—

Must I forever be
Slurred of two faces?
Must I forever see
Kin in two faces?

Christ, if God was white
And Mary, not,
You'd curse the star-stung night
You were begot!

Roman Carpenter on a Good Friday

He came amongst us, labored, and displayed
His quiet knowledge of the Maker's trade.

But how were we to tell the false from true,
How rest a sudden faith in rebel Jew?

And so I made the cross. On Calvary sod
It struck me He looked, bleeding, like a God!

I Dreamed I Was the Lord

My Lord, I dreamed last night of Calvary,
But You stood on the hill, that careless moss
Had overgrown, and turned away from me
Who was left hanging limp upon the cross.

I shudder at the fear with which I died
That no one there would cherish my spirit's flame;
But most of all the spear that pricked my side
Was the knowledge you did not even know my name.

I shall not soon forget that dream, My Lord,
Not soon forget my instant in your place,
Not ever be unmindful of your Word,
Nor that I bore a moment your sad face.

Our mutual cross binds us so tight today
That neither of us, now, can turn away!

Peter

Peter was troubled by his friend's calm face.
What Peter heard was "I go in thy place."

And as they took Peter's friend away,
A frown stilled what Peter had to say.

His friend, twice-dying, became ever-living,
But Peter was stranger to quick forgiving.

Christ never knew his careless frown
Crucified Peter upside down!

Mass Crucifixion

Once a crucifixion
builded up great spires
wherein a dying benediction
was repeated to the crucifiers
through long dark ages
until a race was saved.

With the spirit's wages
a golden road was paved.

But the gold is pounded thin
and at the road's ending
there is no letting in . . .
only a quick descending,
and the spires—once more than symbol—
are symbol now and nothing more.

From a meagre and unquenching thimble
rather than flowing cup, the waters pour.

Once a cross with burden nailed
left a people's vision full
of a glory and a faith that prevailed
like what it was, a miracle;
and in the later, darker years
Golgotha was sacred memory.

But now the spirit's tears
would flood a bitter sea.

Crucifixions matter little
and spires house but misers' rooms;
only the jot and tittle
of expense incurred for martyrs' tombs
are given any thought
by wholesale crucifiers.

Bone and flesh, as needed, are bought
while souls are dropped on systematic pyres.

Deep in the viscera of earth,
the thousands crucified—
not once but every day from birth—
doomed to die as their fathers died,
begin to raise a question
that makes their senses reel:
"Is all of life this Earth—Digestion—
man macerated to faeces of coal and steel?"

And on the earth's crawling hide
masses decide they are not vermin,
so they commence to deride
each silver-underwritten sermon
that begs them to go forth again
and scratch a pitiful content.

The masses quick find that masses are men
and loose the cry a century pent.

The cry is amplified
like thunder through the nation,

the volume swollen by those who died
of hunger for man's salvation,
and the wraiths of the dead
incense the wrath of the living.

And in no thorn-pricked head
is there an atom of forgiving.

So on some soon tomorrow
there shall come to earth at last
surcease of intolerable sorrow,
surcease of sackcloth and of fast,
when each horizon shall fulfill
the promise of a thousand trysts.

And man shall reap the multi-miracle
of benediction
for the crucifixion
of a million nameless Christs!

Selected Poems 1943-1974
I. Personal Journal

The Deaf
(For My Father)

Out of the darkness, out of the years, out of the
    mind's reluctant hoardings,
faintly the whisper reaches, then recedes, faintly
    the sound describes a circle
far out of reach. Caught on the perilous edge
    of vague concentric impulse,
the ears, spread tight against the precipice of
    hearing, precariously pluck a tremor
that seems to be more memory than sound. Here is
    adventure set to music
yet unheard, or heard too many seasons past; here
    is a wall
that needs quick climbing, or that was climbed too
    long ago. Or maybe it is no wall
at all. Perhaps this looming obstacle to understanding
    is sound unfiltered;
perhaps a strained attention yet will capture the fine
    elusive fugitive
of sound that hovers out of reach. We clench the hand,
    we bulge the jaw,
we wince and arch, yet bring the trembling wings of
    distant, or imagined, noise
no nearer, no slightest line's width nearer.

Out of the darkness, out of the years, out of the
    mind's reluctant hoardings,
comes what the braver know is memory; comes what the
    craven try to think
is tangible and present and recorded against the
    futile tightened drums
that hold their thinkings taut. Out of the darkness, out
    of the years, out of the mind's
invincible and fearless voyagings, the braver find
    a quiet place,
a peace that mountains have, or seas, or clouds, to

    find themselves against a sky
that they may never touch. The braver go, happy in
    sight of birds
that fly with silent whirr, or brooks that have a
    silent splash, or boys that play
wildly in loud quiet. Out of the darkness, out of
    the years, out of the silent
orchestration minds can make, the braver march to
    a silent air,
lifting their eyes to the curious banners that crackle
    in silence, and watching their pennons
furled proud then whipped aloft by a silent wind.

Artist and Ape

I stand before your cage to make my sketch,
catching in line and shade your jungle look,
your hate of man, your willingness to play
his little game for food and drink, your hope
that someday he will lose his wariness
and come too close. I make my pencil move
in ways I do not altogether fathom
and here on paper see your fingers tight
around steel bars you someday mean to bend.

Your eyes upon the paper somehow show
fury and fright and lust that were not there
before I started work. The sketch takes shape
limning a creature (the idle thought occurs)
with more of man in him than many men
my pencil knows. And suddenly I want
to tear it off the pad, to make confetti
against the wind, to sow a thousand parts
of paper ape upon an earth that spawns
too many apes already. But art or the Devil
lurking behind the bush prevents the gesture.

And anyway the sketch is good . . . too good.
I look into your eyes once more and wonder,
should I say "Thank you, Ape," for posing well,
for showing me the depths to which man sinks
or whence he came? Or should I turn away
as if you were a model paid to stand
twenty minutes while my pencil made
mock of the paper's virgin awareness?

Those deep-set, beady surfaces give stare for stare;
my spine feels the little mice of history
run up and down with frozen feet. I shrug,
try not to shudder, then twist around and jot
the date in lower left-hand corner.
                              A pause.
What title shall I write across the top?

The picture, lecherous and frightful, names itself:
boldly I scrawl the descriptive phrase—"Self Portrait."

Grammarian's Grave

They told me you were dead. I went to see
if any words on carven stone could be
correct, precise and cold as your living speech.
I found four words: "He lived to teach."
"To teach?" I asked, and all about me nouns
panted their answers; camouflaged in browns
and reds and greens, they still were naked, shamed
pathetic fallacies at heart. Maimed
phrases staggered across a tongue so used
to measure sound they were stiff, bemused
finding freedom. Something about your dying
seemed to loosen a caged bird, set it flying

in my thought. Here was a noun declined forever,
the noun of you; here was your life's endeavor

falling to dust at the touch of original thinking
(mixing a metaphor is much like too much drinking
if your viscera's not trained for it). Bright
as Bikini's artificial sun the light
of verbal liberation washed the scene
flooding my mind. I hummed a daring keen
and tapped a foot against your firm, dry mound.

Suddenly a firm, dry voice disturbed the ground
crying: "Who dares to dance upon my grave?"
and I, one foot in air, too newly brave,
could not decide because too newly free
whether to say "it's I" or else "'it's me."

Capillary Signpost

Thermometers do not concern the heart;
A martial drumming shakes its tight-stretched wall
In frost and thaw, in greening spring, in fall
At any call to arms. The blood will start
Pounding its overtures of love or war
In scorn of Centigrade and Fahrenheit!

The stimuli of hate, desire, fright
Are not amenable to metric score.

The heart can climb the throat in hot assault
While snow berimes the windows of the mind;
And pulse may pause in veins that ice has lined,
Facing in summer sun a carven vault.
Beware quicksilver tubes that men contrive
Telling to what degree they are alive!

The Leader

The strong winds blew across the land, the loud
crash of debris was heard wherever man
looked around bewildered. The strong winds blew
in the high places. The walls shook . . . and men's hands,
wherever there were walls and men. The winds
of hate and fear blew strong across the land.

And men prayed for a leader to shore their walls,
to fend the winds, to bring them safe across
the menacing plains, up the mountains of hope.

And a leader rose. He strode across the land
nine feet high and four feet wide and cast
a shadow that loomed as high as the mountains and long
as the land itself. When he waved his arms the skies
darkened, the enemy quaked, opponents froze.

His eyes were bright and his voice was soft but he strode
nine feet high and four feet wide and held
the fate of the world in his hands. But the strong winds
blew across the land, the winds of hate,
the winds of fear—and like an underswell
somehow the opposition grew in strength,
somehow the enemy lost his fear and men
talked of war and ruin. The strong winds rose
and the Leader felt them rise in his high place;
he felt them pluck at his sleeves and nip at his ankles.

The day came when the shutters slammed against the walls
of the Leader's house. The wide doors blew open—
the winds of hate and fear grew loud and hard.

The Leader leaned against the winds, he spread
his arms across the wide doorway, standing
nine feet high and four feet wide, but shaken
and sudden the winds plucked off the Leader's coat,

the winds of hate and fear snatched at his trousers,
pulled them down about his giant boots.

And the palace guard stared up in fright to see
an angry little shock-haired boy on stilts
with a wide kite-frame strapped firm to his puny shoulders.

The Leader, used to striding, took one step
and fell to the ground, but the winds of hate and fear
cushioned the sound except for those nearby
already walking away, not looking back.

The Color of Danger

i

Danger was green; through the jungle where the bamboo
reached up long, and endlessly elbowed arms to hold the
                                                            sky back
and twined its infinity of fingers across the sky's face
to keep all blue away, men staggered up to their hips
in the undergrowth of a million pagan years;
men crawled on their bellies up the slime of so many oozing
                                                            river banks
that crawling became a way of life and standing up at last
seemed ponderous and difficult.

And every minute out of the dank green
came the fetid breath of messengers long dead trying to say
"Go back, drop everything, this is not the way,"

And flesh that the green touched soon became no flesh
                                                                   at all,
flesh that was punctured by unseen unheard missiles
fulfilled its ultimate mission—
to fertilize the place of danger.

ii

Danger was white; the land had no believable existence;
only history knew that land like any other land
lay long since locked in ice long miles below
the place where they slept and woke and fought
and had their monochrome, their one-dimensional being.

Men who seemed to roll across the now, so round they were
with woven armor, deft cocoons against the cold,
carried their weapons smoking with the frost
like menacing blue stalactites
across the rolling frozen plains, up the frozen glass ravines.

Suspended motion, time incalculable
over crevice no man could leap and live . . .
and suddenly the film takes motion, the figure springs from
                                                               its still exposure,
lands on the edge it could not reach
and rolls away across horizons frozen into place.

Danger was white; yesterday or this afternoon or tomorrow
they did not reach the iced horizon; they slipped back down
                                                                 ravines,
their fingers turning their woolen mittens red.
the little drops of blood spelling out upon the lower snow,
"Go back, drop everything, this is not the way?"

And flesh that the white touched soon became no flesh at all;
flesh that was punctured by bombs of overhanging ice,
by little frozen bullets from blue-white metal birds,
fulfilled its ultimate mission—to occupy the icebox of the
                                                                 ages,
food for the gods of frozen future time.
Danger was white; it breathed a mist across their faces,
it whispered whitely of death.

iii

Danger was blue; blue deep and blue far
and coming in myriad maritime shapes;
men did their appointed tasks as calmly as if their tilting
                                          precarious feet
were posted firm upon the good firm earth.

Well-groomed carefully accoutred ants, they scurried
when danger was translated from color to sound,
the edge of blue gathering itself into little tufts of darker
                                          blue and gray
upon the stage of the horizon and merging with sirens and bells to make
                                          curious blue noise.

Danger came by day, by night, and in the thin time that was
                                          not either,
the blue lightnings playing up and down and around the ship.
their fingers edged in red flame writing upon the sanded decks,
"Drop everything, run, jump into the sea, this is not the way."

But men cannot read at sea in time of battle,
they do their little appointed tasks;
they die, but a turret has been mounted;
they paint the scuppers a blue red with the pigment of living,
but a whistle has been blown, a lanyard pulled, a signal flag
                                          fluttered
against the blue of danger.

iv

Danger was black; out of the night a sowing of black seeds
                                          in the bitter earth
that leapt to sudden crimson flowers, petals of explosion,
                                          stamens of death;
out of the night came the quick black fingers with flaming claws
to scratch a message in the blank spaces of a man's mind,
"Go back, drop everything, this is not the way."

And flesh that the black touched soon became no flesh at all,
fulfilled its ultimate mission—to blacken and dry and go
                                            to powder
and blow away upon the dark winds into the night.

But somehow men remained fixed, afraid, and firm in the dark,
waiting the sight and sound and smell and feel of danger,
and danger was black.

v

What is the color of danger then?
Danger is all colors to all men.

When danger was young it had a magic color,
when danger was ripe it had a mysterious shade;
when danger was old it had a curious half-remembered, half-
                                            forgotten tinge;
but it has never disgarded color old or new;
it hoards all shades that men have put to it
or named or thought or painted.

Danger is polychrome; it walks in many colors
to insure that men perceive it though they be color blind;
the eye that holds no red can call no halt,
the eye that holds no green calls no advance;
but danger is all colors to all men.

When man goes off to war he must resolve to drink all
                                            colors in,
to take them in his pores by dark, by light,
to breathe them in like air, so danger may permeate him,
become part of his being;
he must himself be danger,
be danger everywhere.

The Golden Eagle

When I was small a golden eagle perched
atop a mountain crag, a special place
that held my dreams for me to study them.

The eagle whirring off seemed to take
my dreams along. And I would race below
matching his light through the length of the valley.
But he always got smaller and smaller and disappeared
seeming somehow to take my dreams along.

Now I am grown—grown more than grown—
grown old, and still I chase my dreams
with the golden eagle flying high above,
but higher, smaller than ever.

Or else I run along the valley slower
stopping more often to catch my breath,
clutching my heart—
the dreams are gone farther away in space;
the golden eagle flew faster
then I could ever run.

Minor Variations of the Theme of Dogwoods

i. ACCIDENT

I hold the reins of ten horses in my hand
as I sit in my chariot mowing machine.
I am the high-riding master of the land
and all things green;
the scrub stands short, the grass rolls flat
wherever I steer.

Then suddenly I loosen the reins and veer
a foot off course . . . too late I haul the slack
and try to pull my monster back.

Too late. The wheels of my chariot
have rolled the length of a dogwood tree;
its three-year trunk lies prone
upon the ground. I leap down with a visceral groan;
the body stays still, its roots frayed out and torn.

But I cannot stop to mourn . . .
I dash to the shed and chop a pole in two,
then pound the oaken shaft
deep in the earth where the tortured fibers grew,
knowing my actions daft;
I raise the dogwood, lash it firm to the crutch
thinking I feel some movement at my touch:
I press the earth around the base
trying to force new life into the hole
that I cannot face,
feeling empty blossom eyes stare into me.

I turn away dragging my axe along the ground;
as I go, there is no sound
but I wince at the silent scream of a dying tree.

ii. STRUGGLE

Seven red October leaves
clung to my dogwood tree.

The winds of fall came ruffling through
and still they held their grip.

The third day of watching I decided
they must have names to be remembered by.

I called them by the days of the week
and lay awake that night wondering
which would be the first to go.

Strangely it was "Monday";
then, once I turned my back
and "Tuesday" and "Wednesday" were gone.

So I was left with four companions
to fight against winter's charges.

A few days later when I woke
I saw that only one was left—
"Sunday" against all odds!

Day after day my one leaf held—
held to the branch and held with me to autumn.

One night I felt a sudden thump
and thought my heart had stopped;
I lay there cold and somehow frightened.
Next morning all the world was white
and "Sunday" lay upon the snow
like a spill of blood.

Professor's Office

This hour we will consider
ambivalence (or one of us will;
I question if you know the word.)

Meanwhile I must lecture you on form . . .
(parenthesis here for pleasant connotations)
on form in verse.

You have developed (parenthesis: exclamation point!)
in nineteen years the bold, insufferable conviction
that you can do no wrong (parenthesis: in self expression).

Not your father (Ted Roethke reminds me), I cannot be stern;
not your lover (parenthesis for wishful fantasies),
so not demanding.

I walk the cautious line
that puts my cerebral hemispheres worlds apart,
maintain my balance with a teetering strain
that you can never be aware of,
hiding from all eyes
my tense dichotomy.

(Pleasantly firm—this is my watchword);
I tell you how this should go and that should be
(parenthesis: I never knew how many verbs
had copulative implications!)

The hour is suddenly gone,
you gather up your books and turn to leave.

I hold your coat—it's made of strange material:
sixty percent polyester
and forty percent incest.

My Hereafter

Moslems leave this life happy
>   knowing that soon they will live again
>   in luxury with all the sensual delights
>   they have always dreamed of.

Jews know that somewhere Jehovah
>   awaits them to administer justice
>   in the nebulous hereafter.

Christians spend their lives
>   certain their heaven will leave them

        their basic minds and bodies
        unchanged except for the absence
        of stress and strain and suffering.

But as for me—I have a secret
        thought about my own future:
        I will be free and bright and able
        to help people in my new world.

I who have been earthbound will live
        in a boundless watery domain,
        wise in the ways of my new existence.

You will see me from time to time, bursting
        the boundaries between water and air,
        making parabolas against the sky.

You will think that I remind you a little
        of someone that you knew, maybe—
        my joy in my new freedom, maybe—
        my affection for people, maybe—
        what looks a little like a smile
        that you knew, maybe. My name
        will be Dolphin.

Age

One penalty of growing old
        is to read the obits daily
hoping to feel a twinge
        at the news that this one
        or that has passed away;
hoping that this one day
        there will be no joy
        that I have survived, not they.

Another is to watch
    the slow irrevocable
    sagging of chins and bellies
    I look upon, the wrinkles
    multiplying on faces seen each day,
    old friends looking more like
    my father's friends than mine.

Seeing the dark shadow
    over every head,
    watching that man I know so well
    but whose name I can't recall;
    he looks so much like
    someone long remembered,
    but so gray, so tired, so old, so shadowed;
    he looks at me with a vague surmise.
I turn away damning all public mirrors.

In Memorium (F. D. R.)

Thinking of earth's new loneliness
Rather than mine,
I pray for solace
not for me, your lonely neighbor,
But earth herself greatly bereft,
Greatly alone and maybe
Greatly doomed.

Thinking of earth's new emptiness
With you beneath it,
I walk to the highest places
Not knowing where nor how
And lean against the wind
Not seeing
And hear no sound.

Silver Lady

I left you, Silver Lady,
And I danced behind the moon,
And shouted crazy ballads
Quite innocent of tune.
I hurdled over lamp posts
And ducked to miss the stars;
I laughed with glee and overturned
A dozen trolley cars.
I trod upon the moon beams
And mounted to the skies
And was amused, on meeting you,
To note your quick surprise.
I found you, Silver Lady,
In the place where you belong.
You were making of the moonlight
The music for my song.

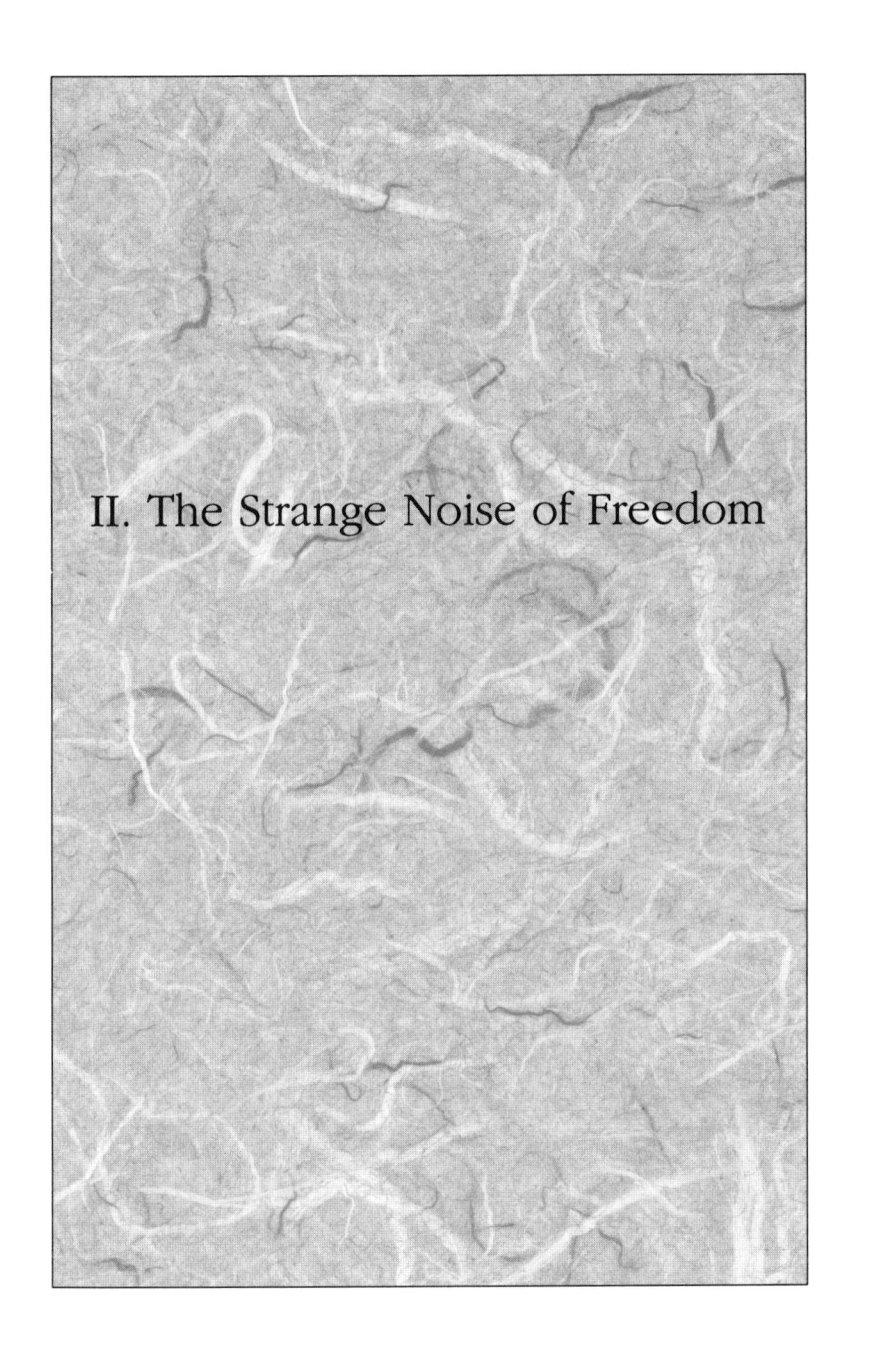

II. The Strange Noise of Freedom

The Strange Noise of Freedom

i

This is the strange noise of freedom,
> beating its subtle drums in the ears of a nation,
> charging the battery of everybody's pulse,
> leaping over city and plain and mountain and ocean
> like the ghost of a million prairie fires.

Stop where you are and listen:
> listen to the traffic noises and the birds
> and the winds in the lonely trees and the tides on the
> > empty beaches . . . .
> listen to the wheels turning and the bells ringing and
> > the weird
> electric sounds across the world
> from a thousand copper-wire spider webs
> that bind the hemispheres in willing subservience
> to the impatient gods of communication.

Listen to the thunder that man is making
> in hope to stay the storm of war forever,
> listen behind the major mood of battle to the thin
> antiphony that rises surely.

Listen to the deafening but unheard rumble
> ten million hearts are making because they beat
> as one great heart in their one great hope
> that beating in a thousand far-off foreign places
> they beat a pattern to bring them home once more.

ii

At home . . . in the subway, the many-hearted animal, the mob
> presses upon itself and bruises its million ribs,

       panting, groaning, shouting, striking out blindly
          upon its myriad-instepped, multi-elbowed self . . . .

A hand in the small of the back and a good-natured shove
       to close a door that must be curved to close,
       to render portatable what cannot move,
       to stand five men upon one set of toes . . . .

A hand in the small of the back and a shout,
       "Watch the doors . . . step lively, mister . . .
       watch your step, sister."

This is the noise of freedom.

And a banker gets mad and socks a guard . . . .
       "I couldn't help it, Your Honor, it got me mad . . . .
       he shoved me in and I got mad and socked him."

And the Judge smiles and the court explodes in laughter
       (and the guard and the banker shake hands there–
          after . . . .)

This is the strange noise of freedom.

iii

In Marrakech, in Anzio, in Brest, in Calais,
       in Tarawa, in Guam, in the Carolines, in Leyte,
       replacements come by air with news and strength
          from home.

They are grasped by their hands, their sleeves and clutched,
          they are smothered,
       and questions patter their ears like eager rain:
       "how are the Brooklyn Dodgers doing?"
       "where will the pennant go this year?"
       "does Louis still make those double hamburgers?"

"how's the beer?"
"are the skirts getting shorter?"
"how are the grinds and the bumps at the Gaiety?"
"what's it like to lie for an hour in a white tub full
of hot water?"
"what's it like to walk down Broadway . . . down Main
Street . . . down Hick's Crossing?"
"what's it like on any street?"
"what' s it like at home? "

*This is the Babel that free men make, this is the noise of
 freedom.*

iv

They walk into battle with a strange wild music in their
        heads,
    they walk into battle from New York, from New Haven,
        from New Rochelle, from New London,
    from San Diego, San Francisco, San Antonio, from
        Santa Cruz, from Santa Fe,
    from all the new world towns with old world names
        across the three thousand miles,
    they walk into battle with the hot winds of victory
        blowing through their hair.

They march and they run and they creep into battle through
        forests
    where the tall trees fall screaming in flames
    over beaches where sheets of molten metal sever the
        waves of cold gray sea,
    over mottled mountains and pock-marked deserts,
        through mud and ice and swamp
    where the skies hurtle down in frightening red-hot
        pieces
    and the earth raises bitter flowers of explosion.

And they fall with the high winds blowing about them,
>   with their spines afire and a mad music in their ears.

The strange noise of freedom sounding in their ears.

v

In Paris Sherman tanks rolled through the Arc de Triomphe
>   bearing a motley burden of tired troops and laughing
>>   girls
>   and hungry children and wine and roses and liberty.

Some were there who spared ironic smile to note that these
>   symbolic juggernauts
>   were named after the man who, fighting to free a nation
>   laid half of it waste, broke half its heart.

But Frenchmen wept aloud and danced and sang
>   and this was freedom's song.

Then for a curious moment as the flags went by
>   Paris was still. As the flags went through the arch
>   no word was said, no shout was raised,
>   no horn was blown and no child cried.

And this was the noise of freedom.

vi

After a thousand days of war a million men
>   have found their ways once more to the million homes
>   that they were fighting for and now they know
>   a painful pride in home and love and liberty
>   that once they took for granted like the air and skies
>>   and stars.

They walk their olden, newly-savored ways,
    they go to work on trains and buses,
    they point toward home at five o'clock
    and they read and rest and play and vote.

A man who lived in foxholes for the right
    makes a little ritual of voting.

The swish of a curtain as he locks himself secure within a
        polling booth
    and raises the little lever that balances the fate of the
        world,
    the moment's hush before he pulls the lever down,
    when he probes his mind once more,
    the mesh of cerebral gears the while he poises
    upon the precipice of ultimate decision,
    and then the sudden falling motion as the die is cast
    and the ballot with it . . . .

These combine to make the curious noise of freedom.

vii

Wherever presses roll and newsboys shout,
    wherever men in jail can get bailed out,
    wherever on a corner in any town
    three men can meet and shout each other down,
    this is the noise of freedom in the ears.

And this is the noise of freedom in the heart:
    when a man and wife stand over a map and view it
    and say, "We'll stick a pin in it and then we'll start
    wherever we find the pin" . . . and then they do it!

The pin makes infinitesimal sound to plumb the chart
    at any given point—Atlanta as it happens—
    but this is the noise of freedom . . . for they go,
    making a glad invasion down Peachtree Road.

And next year, maybe, they'll go to New Orleans,
    or Hollywood even, or maybe even Paris!

And they'll leave a note for the milkman on the porch
    and the sound it makes as he pulls the note
    out of the empty bottle and reads it smiling
    and the early morning tune that he hums in his throat
    and his steps on the walk as he leaps back to the wagon
    and the surreptitious crinkle the curtain makes
    when their next-door neighbor peeps out to make certain
    that they have really gone . . . these make a mighty
        sound.

These will make a noise on the records of history.

Listen, the strange pervading noise of freedom!

Land He Fought For

PROLOGUE

There is no color line on charts that show
    the way the battles go;
    only a sign to mark the number dead
    in taking of Hill So-and-So;
    and this most useful sign is red.

There are no Jim Crow lorries in combat zones;
    and all men's bones
    tend, when bleached, to turn a sickly white;
    their hearts, exposed to air and light,
    display a common blackness; stones
    or rifle butts or wooden crosses that cry
    "here lies item, private, one, name Doe,
    killed in action twenty-six July

      nineteen sixty-five,"
      do not specify
      "item, shaded so-and-so
      when last inspected, state: alive."

When ground is fertilized with flesh and blood
      and bone of fallen men,
      the flowers rising from the nourished mud
      do not evade the sun and brood
      on the color of sacks the mulch was carried in.

War is no game of chess in echelons
      below General Staff;
      no separate squares for charge of separate pawns;
      often black knight with a curious little laugh
      jumps to an alien spot—white's king square . . .
      and we bury him there.

Endless rows of black knights moved to check
and found themselves laid neatly off the board,
nested in boxes no one soon would open;
but a million others moved from square to square
helping to take the pawns they moved against,
helping to win a game they vaguely understood,
knowing somehow that the game was good.

But war is not a game of chess except
in some habiliments and names and tactics;
motives for war lie deeper, men who move
like pawns on other pawns have more than grain
of hardened wood shaping their fragile skulls,
have more than inner capillary action,
have thoughts and dreams and hopes, have sad conviction
that when they die, they die to make their world
better for sons to live in, safer for dreams.
They die in vain. They do not help themselves,
nor help their sons, nor help the dreams of their daughters.

The million others moved from square to square,
from board to board, and there's the end of chess
for symbol; the thing they were, the thing they bore
in mind and heart, the small excited speech,
in crooning song, and on the point of their steel
was sign enough.

    And George White knew a pride
like a chill clean saber resting along his spine
that he was one of these and that this fight
was personal with them. He felt the rhythm
battle brought to all their movements. Music
was in his thinking. It pressed the color out.

There is no color line in combat zones;
but a wild barbaric music was everywhere;
it reached behind the memory of man;
it carried George from day to singing day
and month to month. And George was myriad.

George White was there. They moved into battle strong
in their faith that only the battle stood between
hope and achievement. Hope survived to die
in peacetime traffic incidents at home,
in barroom shouts by "Hundert P'cent Amurcans, "
in sneers and in hunger. George White discovered this.

Sing this song, put it in your textbooks
with Christopher Columbus and Ponce de Leon:
    "In Nineteen sixty-eight George White discovered
    the land that he had fought for."
                                      Add a footnote
or parenthesis to say "It was not good. "

III. People

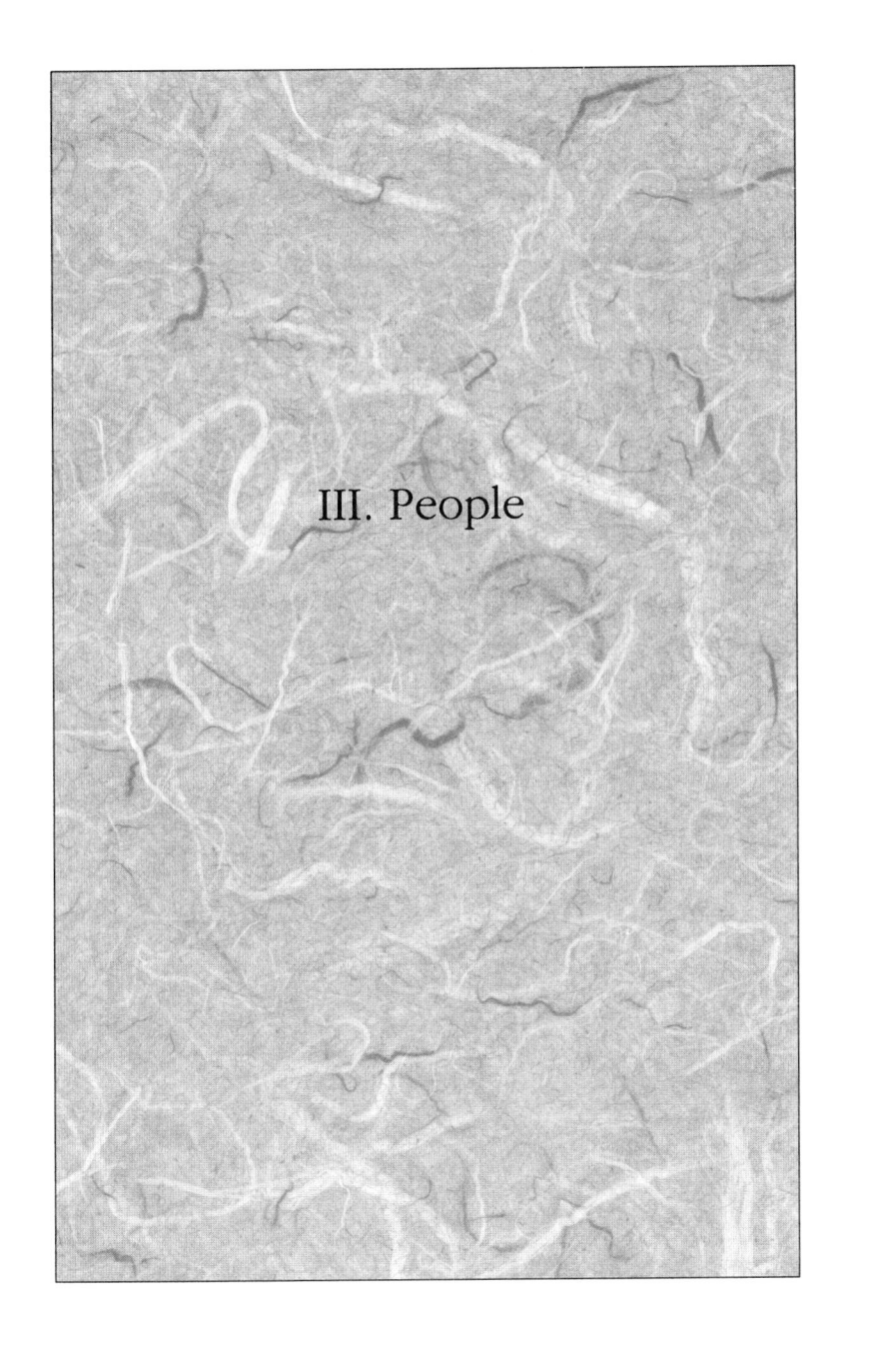

Anonymous Obit

In the small sad room
five men were standing;
each of them mourned a departed friend.
One wiped white tears from his white cheeks,
another let black tears course his black skin;
standing near, a yellow man
made furrows for his yellow tears;
the brown man next to him bowed down
letting the brown tears fall heavy;
and in the corner a red man stood—
one of the tearless race, he shed
slow tears that were clearly red.

Reports do not tell us who it was
the five men mourned; we only know
five tissues found upon the floor
had dried without a trace of color.

Nothing more.

Services for the Dead: A Minor Greek Tragedy

The body in the open bier, separated
by a kind of Aeschylean distance from the throng,
generates in all the compulsive mourners
the twin emotions of pity and fear that Aristotle
first discerned in audiences. Pity
they feel for anyone brought low, and fear,
a pounding fear, that they might fare the same.

The two reactions merge (most of the mourners
never heard of Aristotle's notion):

into *catharsis*, purging them to face the sun,
free of their brief disturbance in the small,

dark, tragic theatre where the stage was shared
by the *Chorus* (a single actor garbed in black)
and protagonist in deathmask, silent, supine.
They face the day in a kind of manic pride
that they hide in chatter and good fellowship.

They did not come to mourn their silent friend;
they came to celebrate their own survival.

My Failing Student
(Now at Arlington National Cemetery)

Rest easy now who had no rest for long;
take from the earth the strength it did not give
while you were quick. There is no right or wrong,
no "shall" or "must," no scowled imperative
to harry your days or make insomniac
your tight-stretched nights where you lie still at last.

Knowing this, we would not have you back
to die each day, each hour, in the perilous, vast
chartless kingdom of the untrained mind. You fought
longer than others have, the unseen foe,
his endless waves of shock troops, panic wrought,
the never-quite arriving final blow

Rest easy now among the many slain
fighting in many wars the same campaign.

Lecture by a Visiting Poet
(For Stephen Spender)

And after he had spoken he signed his name
on books and pads and little scraps of paper,
making his muscles move in cheeks that wished
to fall away in gentle planes of stone,

making the hands perform the friendly task
that would have sought a questionable peace
folded together on chest that did not move;
knowing inchoate haste to be away
from the blurring well-intentioned Torquemadas
who fashion rack and screw of chattering praise.

> (Poets, he'd said, were victimized by times
> that they could write about but not affect;
> between his words fear's loud hiati screamed
> "Who holds the mirror to life's gaped mouth today
> will see no mist upon it, will see clear glass.")

He broke away, I barred his path, I stood
high on my toes and whispered my name in his ear
but knew that he heard only the toll of bells;
he looked at me but plainly saw disaster,
he touched my hand but plainly felt chill
fingers of premonition fluttering about.

e. e.

you were the apotheosis of the lower case,
the highest priest of the bold syllable's
secret dichotomy. your passion was,
and was to be, unpunctuate as humming.

but yours was an esoteric door that left
the key dangling on an obvious hood outside.

for those who chose to use it there was suddenly
only a blur of door that swung wide open.

a man might rejoice as marquis in his own domain
where endless mental commas and quotes and colons
could be dispensed at will, or letters raised,

or tortured syllables made whole, or clauses
pulled up short by the traffic sign of dot.

now may the Proof Reader checking your last page
slyly mark a "stet" on every line
and end an era with an exclamation point!

A Memory of Dark Hair

My mother never plucked a gray hair
from her dark head. She died too young.

Now, at my present age, she could have been
my daughter. But I don't want a daughter.

I want a mother, a little old, white-haired lady
sitting and rocking across the room, happy
and watching me fondly, proud of her graying son.

I bask in the dream image until sudden
light goes on. I look across the room
and on the moving rocker is a carved stone
surmounted by a soft black pompadour.

Old Men

I am kind to all old men I meet; each one
in his peculiar way brings back my father.

One with his straight aquiline nose, another
with pale, blue disappointed eyes,
and all with defeat's hard calipers blackly etched
from nose to mouth. I hang upon their words
and nod agreement my father never knew;
I live with them a past they see so clear,

I spend on them my love's hypocrisy;
they are so like my father except that
their's is a mobile, vague interment above
the ground that keeps my ancestry as still
as Laocoon.
                I am kind to all old men
as I was not when he was one of them.

God bless old men wo bring my father back
and pity me who now am kind from guilt.

English Professor

In this dull class I spend my tired days
Compelling "English themes" that rob my nights
And sap my strength. I claw the humid haze
That thickly chokes the faint and far-seen lights
Of lamps I hope to make each youngster use
Down the approaching years. And no heart sings
In all the little crowd that scuffles shoes
To speed the hour . . . and none has thought of wings
The searching mind can make. I try to tell
Brightly the tales of troubadours and bards,
But the restless buzz is splintered by the bell,
And youth foams forth to cry of "backs" and "guards."

Was I, too, once a thoughtless brawny lad
Who closed his ears and drove a poet mad?

Kansan Poet Far From Home
(An acrostic for Kenneth W. Porter)

Kansas suns poured brown upon your face;
Endless prairies drew your quiet eyes
Nearer the horizon and left a trace
Narrowed there of well-remembered skies.
Every plowing that your youth has known
Tills your cheek with reminiscent joy;
How the soil has claimed for its own,
Weeding your brow to fruitful corduroy!

Perhaps you tire sometimes of the city,
Other parts and other faces calling;
Rather than this extended futile pity,
The chance to still a frightened small calf's
                                      bawling.
Eloquent of Kansas. . .do you roam,
Recalling He was ever far from home?

IV. Places

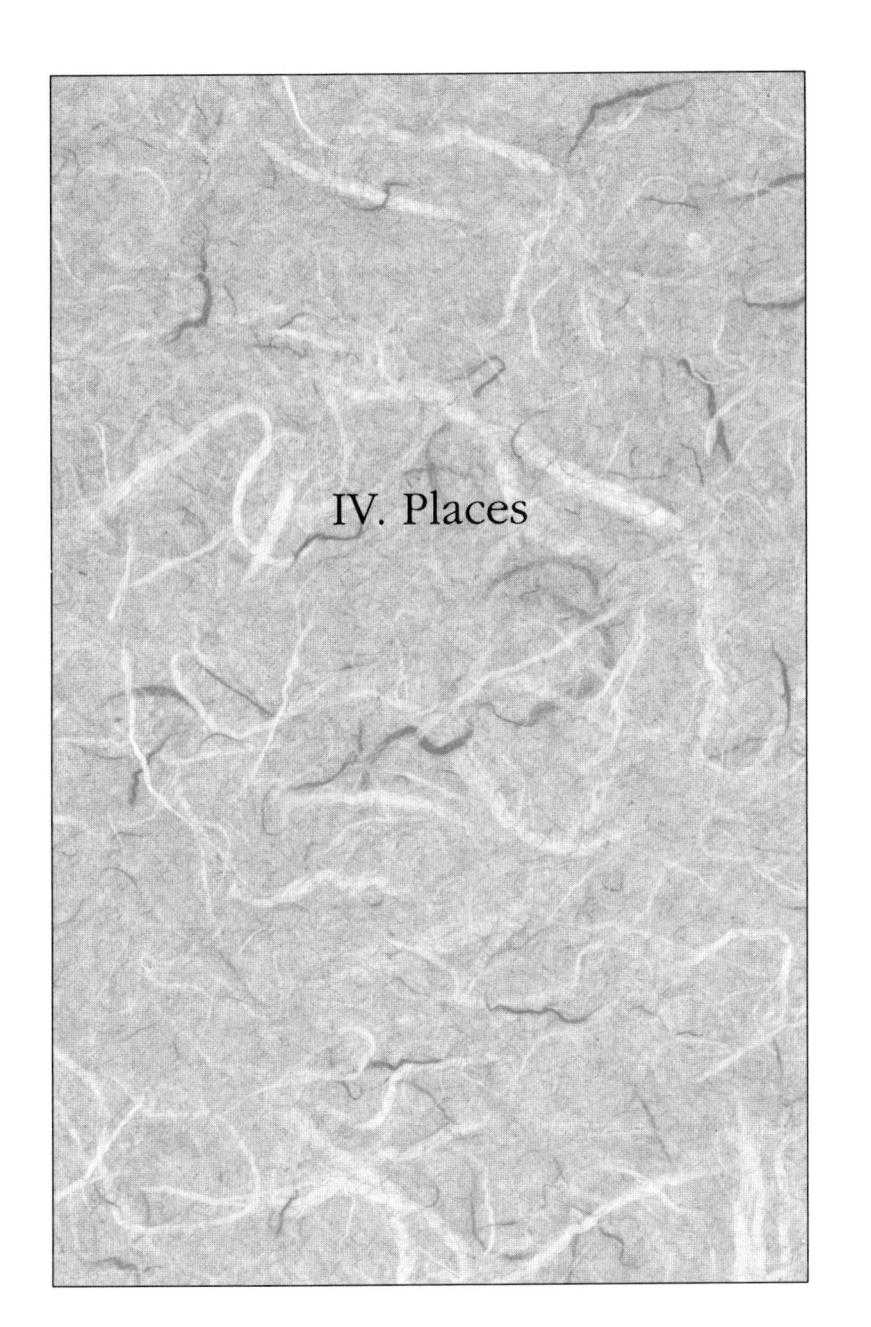

A Pause in Arlington Cemetery

Across the snow I watch the caissons come
Bearing friend whom I have never seen;
Near me a gray memorial carved of ice
Describes another friend with no known name.

As far as my eye can follow the endless rows
Of little stones that barely top the snow
Lie proud beneath the earth the quiet, strange
Soldier congregations now at peace.

Threads that survive the drought and flood and weevil
Men weave to fragile khaki suits of mail
To shield their youth against the blows of evil,
To gird their youth that quests eternal grail.

Beneath the cloth the yielding flesh is all
That men possess for guard against the foe:
When cloth and flesh are pierced a man will fall,
The walls once breached, the futile blood will flow.

Though nameless nightmare weaponries are fashioned
To make war frightening, this tired stone
Argues that man, alive, pierced and impassioned
Succumbed behind this cloth, this flesh, this bone.

Only the dead know peace, for he alone
    May have a certain guarantee of rest
Who bears six feet of earth and carved stone
    Upon the placid marble of his breast;
Who having left all earthly things behind,
Beneath the earth is comfortably blind.

And now the caisson stops. My friend is here:
In the sudden stillness comes another sound:
The wind brushing the snow
    from the round stones.

Touching a cold feather to a wet cheek,
touching the rifle straps, touching a saber.

Friend, you have a special symbol here,
A quick memorial peculiar and your own:
As the guard steps forth, each foot goes down precise—
These marks they make upon the enameled snow
Have not been made by man before. The blue
Chiselled molds form requiem for you.

Snow has a use that men have not before
Observed in song. It bandages the ground
Where bombs or graves have left a running sore;
It makes a curious quilt to dim the sound
Of earth dropping on wood . . .

They come together now at last
    Beneath an earth that oft before
Has buried under a sudden past
    A race, a dream, a hope, a war.

Soldiers do not live alone
    Nor do they die alone.
And this we know of them that here
    They do not lie alone.

        *   *   *

What are the sounds of peace that you have found?
    The muted roll of drums, the creak of leather,
    the scrape of boots in unison, the soft
    snow-muffled, measured clop of a horse's hooves,
    cocking of rifles before the last salute,
    or the textile whisper that comes when a flag is folded?
But here no murmur of mourners, no anguished cry . . .
    only the keen of a cold wind in the frozen trees.

For you come to this last place from far away
    with no one here to see you go. No one?

Every friend you marched with, slept with, fought with
    is here or on his way. And every sound
    you ever knew in uniform, snow-muted now
    combines to make the small proud noise of peace.

    A soldier does not need a crowd of mourners;
    He knows his friends are with him as he lies
    Warm beneath the flag for which he fought.
    Ready to take his place in the welcoming earth.
    Some friends have gone ahead to wait for him
    And some are here to fire off the guns
    That make a symbol sound before he goes
    (For him who fired many guns in life).

And one friend more who stands apart a little
Raises a silver horn and splits the sky
With the purest sound that armies have devised—
The sound of Taps to send their comrade home.

The Round Rocks of Palestine
(Bethlehem, Christmas 1971)

Here where the steps of giants left a tread
That housed the hopes of nations; here where stars
Lighted the fingerprints of God, the scars
In the earth where Mary, weeping, bowed her head;
Here on the slopes of rocky hills where prayer
Could move a stone away, and even mountains,
Conjure loaves and fishes, love and fountains,
Make the cynic scratch his head and stare. . . .

Here where the rocks have rounded aeons past
And history has turned its marble page,
Sometimes the hilltops, sun-blurred, seem to cast
Shadows that emphasize the world's great age.

Deaf to the clash of battle's metal rime,
Here lie the weathered granite skulls of time.

Hospitals

My father's father went to a hospital once—
    in Philadelphia, it was—and died;
my father went to a hospital once—
    in Washington, it was—and died;
my mother briefly knew a hospital—
    in Long Island—and died.

I think of them whenever I visit sick friends
    or make church duty calls; I walk the wards
    and count the coffins resting on steel frames
    covered with blankets and sheets
    to make them look like beds;
    I look into the private rooms
    and note the covered coffins there.

Why do I think of hospital beds
    when I am riding through the night
    enjoying the hum of wheels, the slightly swaying motion?

And why am I lying down while we drive along?
Who are these young men sitting by my side?
"What am I doing here?" I ask.

"It's all right, Pop," a young man says,
    "You're going to the hospital
    and you'll be O.K."

Dubious Conquest

Rockjawed I stand, a little man of rock
upon a thrusting prow of steel, watching
the angry waves recede, the seas divide
sullen to let us through. This ship and I
are each of us endowed with weight enough
to make us plummet down unfathomable fathoms;

but each of us has cunning buoyance the sea
cannot contrive to conquer here and now,
heave though it may with the strain of trying. The long
gray fingers pluck at us, they grope blindly
to get their salt-edged nails beneath our hatches,
under our plates, into our battened ports.

There are perilous moments of fog and foam and almost
overwhelming liquid bulk when the prow
probes deep into breast and tentacles of sea,
into salty gray wet prophecy of doom;
now must the little man of fancied rock
cast his pose aside and grasp at rail,
mouth a sailor's curse, lose hoarded breath.

Then both emerge victorious once more;
the prow cuts proud; the man swears loud, calling
the sea a name that embraces hate in sound
but love in tone . . . and a secret fear in mind.

Here is the enemy that does not want me home,
that fears to let me go, lest sons of mine
if they be born come back to conquer it.

But now, once more a little ship has kept
course on a sea that has not always been
tolerant of rockjawed men, of steel-hulled craft;
safe I stand upon a prow of steel
secure, yet chill of spine remembering
two thousand fathoms drop beneath my feet.

Beneath this shell on which I dare the fates
to thwart my hopes of getting home again,
two thousand fathoms drop to cold dark places
where ships like this have long since washed away
to rusty skeletons . . . and men of rock

were sandstone men not catalytic to the sea's
insistent chemistry.
        And chill of spine
remembering tomorrow. . . and maybe. . . and perhaps. . .

Letter from Cairo (Selection)
(Open Letter to My Wife)

If the rain slant or the mind twist, if the heart be stricken,
 If the eyes wince, or the blood leap, or the fever lines
        rise,

There in my own land, there where my people sing. . .
That is my being. My breath catches and my pulses quicken
To cardiac thunder as I stand, staring into alien skies,

Thinking of home. I burst into a sweat of wanting and my tongue
        begins to cling
To the roof of my mouth and damned but undammable tears rush
        down to burn
The nicked places on my cheek and chin. And while
        they stream,
I cling to the hope of some incredible escape,
Some magic day when somehow I shall suddenly return
Endlessly, drowning my thirsty, long remembering eyes,
Drowning my eyes in long remembered meadows,
To lave away cornea cracks that come from staring
Here in Mena-Giza where nothing is real, where all
        things only seem;
Where the eye retains the shape of endlessly sought for
        shadows;
Where the sun is no friend to signal day and hope, but
        dangerous, glaring
Menace to man. Something in me is baking hard and dry
As the mouth of the Sphinx. What matter history and tales
Of the Bible Land, what matter Cleopatra's barge and my
        billet on the Nile
(Villa 43 which doubtless housed Mark Antony) when
 I would give what's left of me to fly

Straight to Peachtree Road. Instead I press my dehydrated heart
Between the pages of this book I write and send it through the mails.

If the rain slant or the mind twist, if the heart be swollen,
If the eyes wince, or the pulse leap, or the stethoscope be still,
There in my own land, there where my people grew . . .
That is reality, from that may not be stolen
A single thought of mine. If nations rise and kill
Nation on nation a hundredfold and brew
Tempests that rock the world . . . my single thought shall dwell
Only on this: someday I shall return, though I be bone and
                              mummy skin;
And folk who ask about the places I have been,
Who ask me all about what I have seen, why I have fought,
Will hear a curious thing. They will listen perhaps amazed
                              for I shall tell
Proudly the brave and sounding words my father taught
And sing with pride my mother's songs. The sky
Over any town at home that I have known will be

Color for thinking; and all the phrases learned in class
Will rise to ultimate reality in terms of long
Familiar sights and sounds . . . "Atlanta to the Sea."
"Remember the Alamo. " "Fifty-four Forty or fight". . .
The names, the magic names of my incredible land will pass
In magic ways across my mind to make my heart lift strong
Remembering . . . The Ozarks, the Piedmonts, the Blue
                              Ridge; the light
Sifting through Jersey smoke; the River at Nashville and Norwalk;
                              the shore
At Miami, Virginia Beach, and Fire Island . . .
The green light that you have to follow when you take
The shuttle from Grand Central to Times Square; the door
Of Louey's Royal Cafe in Gaffney, smelling of ale;
And beer at the Crimson and Harvard Yard at night
And literary teas in Boston where they give you chocolate cake;
And Wacker Drive and Hollywood Boulevard and the Oregon Trail,
And open roads that you can follow to open places . . .
These knew the pride of my glance, these are in *my* land;

They, and each cannonless border, each undefended lake,
They leave their mark on my brain, they leave their secret traces.

(How can a sudden catalogue explain
The way my heart is grown to flowering clamber-vine
That clutches ten thousand miles of streets and roads and beaches,
That clutches a hundred houses big with love or pain. . . .
The way my memory looks long away and reaches
A needle of ice down my proud straightened spine?)
If the rain slant, the mind twist, the heart be hungry,
If the pulse wane or the spade drop in final earthen token,
There in my own land, there where my people labor,
These have importance, these are the facts of life, these
                                        will make me angry
Or sad or lonely; these will bring hurt to be soothed by a
                                        kindly neighbor
Known all my life. And now that I have said this, now
                                        that I have spoken,
I rise refreshed; I stand and stare impertinent beneath
                                        this alien sun,
Knowing that miracles can happen, that someday I shall run
Once more through meadows, once more shall walk the
                                        breast-tall grasses,
Once more shall be concerned with little things, with all that
                                        passes,
There, there again where rain has more of wet and gleam,
The mind has more of memory and more of thinking,
The heart must swell up greater, the eyes open wider,
To take in all the space my fathers knew in dream . . .
To comprehend a land as quick and free as winking,
As common and fine and clean as apple cider.

Veterans' Hospital

Shaken a little, anchored firm in space
With the stream of time full swollen slithering by,
The tiny mist of hours against my face,

The rain of days, the sleet of weeks, the sigh
Of windy years, and then the brooding lull
When time and space seem joined in what could be
Struggle or mating. And when I try to pull
Out of the stream I know that I am free
Yet cannot move my hands or feet or eyes,
As if quite suddenly a craft set loose
Disintegrates and with the water's rise
Becomes itself a part of sea. I choose
To anchor here forever while the stream
Covers me thinly like water in a dream.

Reunion in Foxhole

The heart does not return from war, it lies
Mulching the sour earth where it has fallen
Serving the ends of nature: all that dies
Must ultimately make for later pollen
More fertile bedding space. The heart remains
Where the blood it knew was pumped upon the ground
Remembering the brief and rubric rains
That beckoned it.
                  From far away the sound
Comes of a body once well known. But wait . . .
The heart perceives that this one is a younger
Than one remembered. Before it can locate
The shape it seeks, there falls a heart much stronger
Upon this nurtured soil. Then both of these
Hope dumb that mankind someday will be wiser—
Will learn that battle burgeons less than trees,
Hearts more if not employed as fertilizer.

V. Things

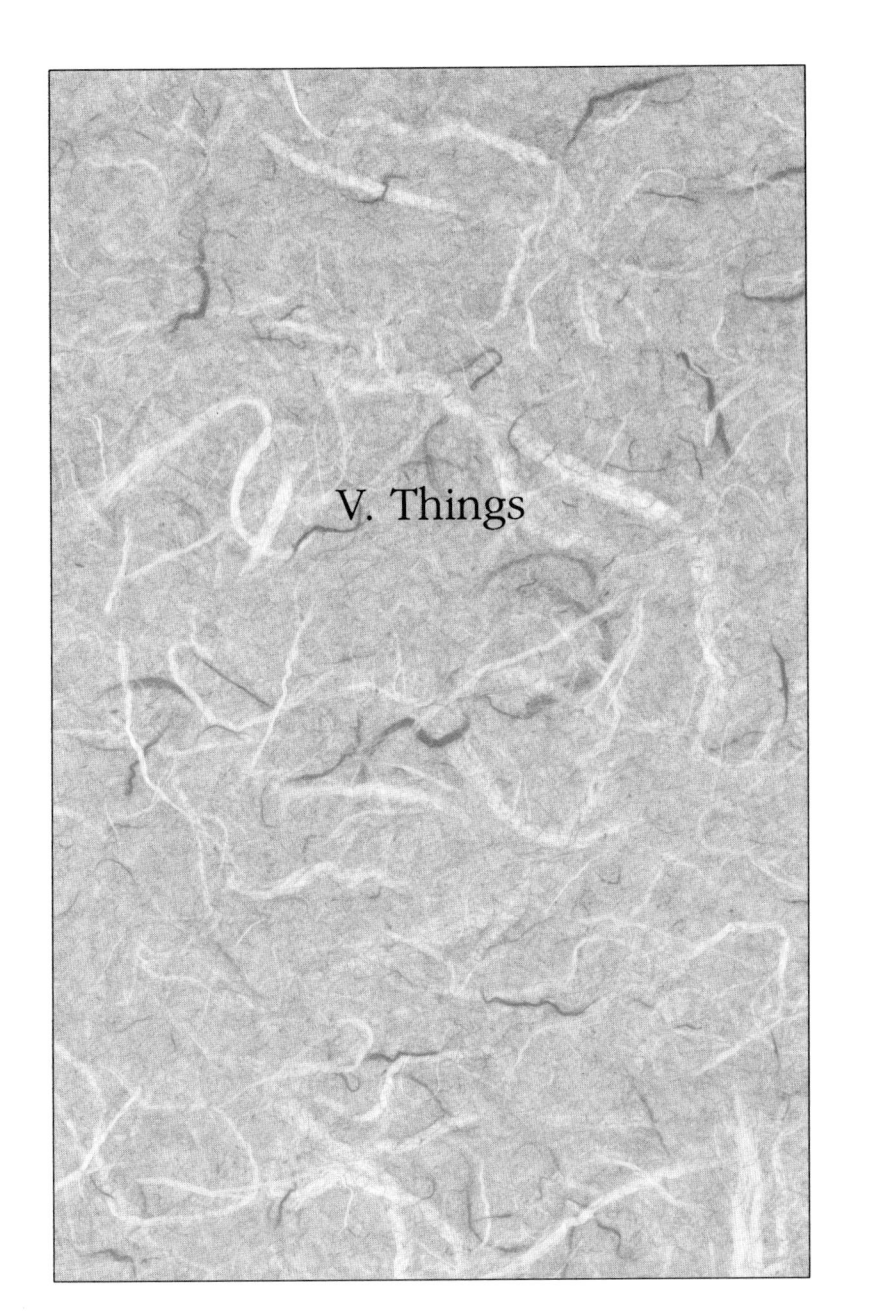

Answer to the Critics of a Poet
(For Jessse Stuart)

What if he utter a word that's used too often,
is he unskilled or cheap because of it?
The meaning, hard, implacable, will soften
and quell to silver stream when squarely hit
only by such or such a sound. And not
of any weight are words themselves except
that it is he who says them. If he jot
phrases on paper they are dialect
of his alone. If we have eyes and nose
the size and shape of someone else's, then
are we forlorn? Do we attempt a pose,
shouting "How common is the face of men!"

What if his words have lived with men before,
perhaps because of this he loves them more!

Frustration

It has taken tired years
Of puzzlement for me to see,
Behind the curtain of my tears
That God has made a fool of me.

He put a hunger in my dreams
For power over mighty throngs;
He filled my brain with worldly schemes . . .
And then He filled my mouth with songs!

Rondeau to Suppressed Ego

"Ich bin ein ich," I tell the sky
Which hovers placid at my cry
And flicks a solitary cloud
In calm derision at my loud

And desperate claim that I am I.

And so the jeering world goes by
While no one deigns to hear my sigh
Although I breathe to every crowd,
"Ich bin ein ich!"

I know not now the reason why
The passerby my words belie,
To no avail how oft avowed.
But someday I, arrayed in shroud,
Shall countersign at Gates on High,
"Ich bin ein ich!"

Staging Area Concerto (Selections)
THE TELEPHONE BOOTH

I stood outside the little booth and thought
it seemed like coffin standing straight on end;
it held, I knew, as much of love and pain
as any buried casket ever did.

For men who entered it at times like this
left life inside, left hope. When emerged
they were automatons, not living men.

What did they say who knew that now perhaps
they heard the voice they loved from far away
for the last time? What could they say? No words
have been devised to travel copper wire,
crossing their fellow words along the line,
and yet make manifest to distant ears,
numb with terror, tense with beat of time,
the simple creed. "I shall return once more."

> "Darling, I shall return again, Darling,
> it won't be long, Darling don't be afraid,

Darling, Darling." The Chinese Nightingale
said this and said this in Lindsay's poem, remember?

Darling, ten years as short as these could not
have 'broke the pattern.' (There's a phrase again
we read together. Amy Lowell's war
seemed far away and quaint.) The pattern's fixed
so firm that I could not escape if even
something in me bid me to, Darling,
I shall come back."

                    And then I, too,
emerged to face the endless line of men
waiting to change their money into sound,
waiting to stumble eager into the booth
and stumble blindly out. To face the truth.

T V

I stare at your oblong, wide curving face
    remembering that nurses tell me I can push
    the button where your left ear should be
    and then your many-colored features
    will turn by magic into pictures of people,
    people making noises with their voices
    and guns and bombs and breaking bones.
And I will hear thunder and see lightning
    and great waves smashing boats against the shores
    and great forests going up in flames
    and buildings crumbling into scarlet embers
    and crowds rioting and armies at war.
And worst of all, the insane laughter
    that people organize behind your back
    when a ventriloquist's dummy named
    Berle or Carson makes noises with his mouth.
These would, if activated, help my sanity when they fade.

I stare at your wide, oblong blank face
     but do not press the magic button. I stare
     and with my hand still poised in air
     I stop and know that I shall never
     reach that far. I am afraid.
     I am afraid . . .

THE PICTURE

The room was van Gogh yellow with the sun
making a golden halo on the glass
of his picture on the bureau.

I left the room thinking how well a halo
fitted him who spent his life in acts
of goodness, in tranquil tones.

I counted his virtues like the beads of a rosary.

For hours I sat on a bench in the park
thinking how sure he was of heaven.

When I returned the room was dark and green;
I opened a bureau drawer, then took the picture down,
removed the frame and laid the glass aside
and neatly stuck three pins
into his saintly heart.

VI. The Edge Of Oblivion

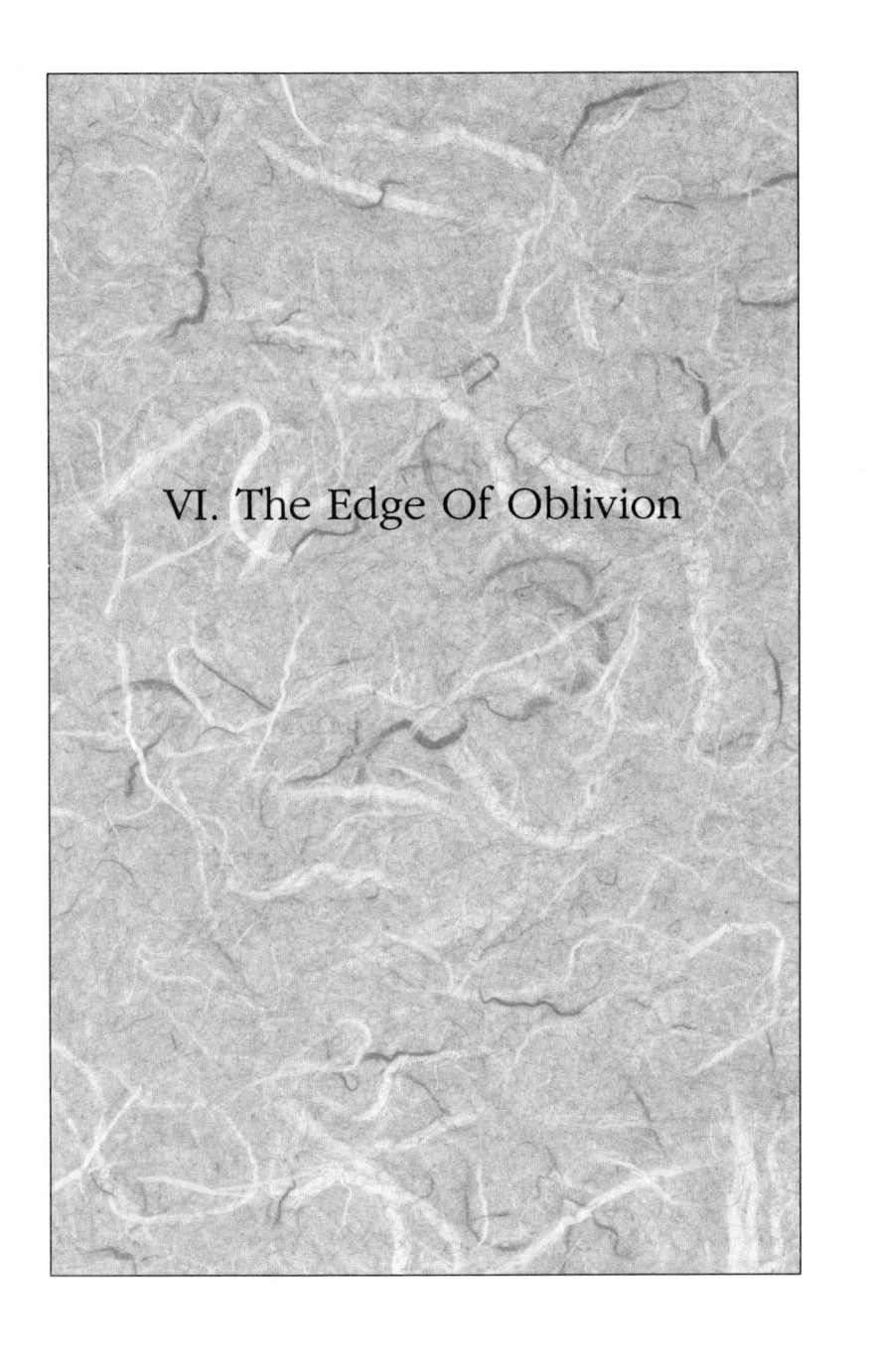

Poetry and Physics

There is minuscule pause
at the junction of four dimensions
when the poem suspends itself in time and space
with abstract edges touching no ganglion's end
or thing or shadow of thinking.

At this infinitesimal delay
in the torrents of time
and the cataracts of curving space
that mate to spawn infinity,
the poem is ignorant of self or form
or destiny or pulse or sound.

It might emerge heroic
from this fractional log jam of history
as sermon or music or design or dream,
and only God who owes His being
Himself to this intricate phenomenon
can know how many poems
stipple our past disguised as symphonies
or steeples or religious revivals
or the staring skulls of dream upon the sands
that bury half-remembered races.

And this is well: if a poem survived
from every impulse man has had
to fossilize himself in song,
our heritage from history would be
mounds of memorial star-high and eternity-wide;
the topheavy would stagger through the dark
uninhibited and cold and doomed
to never ending unawareness of man's capacity
for constructing nonconformist deities,
for translating tribal rhythms into a way of life,
for splitting hairs and infinitives and atoms.

The Little People

From time that has no work, we have been and begot
and made our little noise about little things;
we have never been in the way. We have not
raised our voices about anything important; and our kings
have been kind to us. We have not made scenes . . .
except when over-hungry and then with many small
separate angry shoutings but no united thunder.

We have been prey to wonder
and fear and sloth and the weight that custom leans
against the lifting mind. But most of all,
we have been prey to some archaic spell
cast on us in the ancient dark to make us blind
when leaders came showing the way, giving the word.

They have risen out of the dark, they have spoken
in magic ways to set us free, but we have not heard;
rather we have torn them down, and then we could not tell
what thing possessed us and could not find
moisture for our drouth when the pitcher was broken.

Our little fathers begat them little sons
outnumbering the stars; we were begat
like the fish of the sea, like the seed of the thistle;
begetting was our only talent; our only pride
was that we never buried it. With rocks, then bows,
                              then guns
we fought to propagate the earth; we clotted;
we recapitulated Genesis;
then, taking our myriad turns, we died.
But they birthed us faster than the myrmidons
of the Black Horseman could spring to saddle;
though we died by villages, by towns, by cities,
though we died by tribes and nations and races,
from starving, from eating, in peace, in battle . . .
and, more than passing pity,
most of us left no traces.

If some there were who tried with words
on rock, papyri, parchment, books as dead as they,
to make us think, to make us dream, to make us look at birds,
we drove them off, the ones we did not slay,
and they built them little ivory towers
that henceforth we might never enter in;
and we went earnest, looking level with our noses.

We were the little people, and we spent our little hours
sowing our seed and hoping for the best
and doing our duty and solemnly avoiding sin
and laying wreaths of myrtle and of roses
upon the endless rows of crosses growing
where wars had sown our little brave.
And we never knew the cream of the jest;
we never learned that any slave
is only a little man you keep from knowing
that he is free; we crawled over the skin of the earth
faster than plague and war and ignorance and other natural death
could reap us down; the frightening invincibility of birth
conquered the frightening impermanence of breath.

We could not be killed away, but we remained
the little people of the world, harnessed, chained;
we were just big enough to tread the wheels in the mills,
to blast the coal out of the mines,
to work the furnaces and lathes and kilns,
to crush the grapes and make the wine,
to lay the brick, to fetch and carry.
And for all our swarming and our teeming,
we never took up too much space; we never got in the way;
we managed to clothe and feed ourselves, to marry,
to keep abreast in some vague manner of all seeming
miracles that come when time and space can multiple each other,
and when they told us to, we took up arms to slay,
sometimes uncomplaining, brother against brother.
We have held close to our virtues and our sins

as we invented them or delved them out of the ages;
and we have grown soft, we have grown slack,
we have nurtured paunches and double chins;
no need now for thumbscrews, for rack;
we are amenable to push or shove or printed pages;
we are the little people of history.

But always one mystery:
how we survive, how were we sustained . . .
in the dark hours, through the plagues, through the flights,
through the terrors, through the hungry years,
hounded and beaten, tortured, enslaved, and chained,
what star beckoned in the black nights?
Reaching small windows in the heart's prison,
what star flickered and then stayed firm,
what silver blade of hope cut through fears,
despairs, fatigues, defeats, frustrations,
to point the apotheosis of the worm,
to point a sun not yet but soon arisen?

But louder than explosions made in battle
or conjured out of tubes to burst the peacetime ear
of kings who might be covetous and bold,
comes through the night the terrifying thunder
like hooves of a million herds of cattle
deafening in the distance, incredibly near,
the sound the little people make rallied and uncontrolled.

Among the complacent councils of the nations,
with planned ingratiating smile
the men in togas rise to split a hair
while atoms split upon Bikini Isle
show how the world may soon be torn apart.
Small walls of hate are carefully erected
while whimpering prophetic sounds are left
trembling upon the numb Pacific air
to say that specks of matter neatly cleft—
with studied guile directed—
can tear down piled-up stars and break God's heart.

And here was our curious blunder:
we did not have to wait this long at all;
we did not have to wait until the earth
were poised upon the edge of quick oblivion
before our victory were won.

We might have risen sooner and made our little ball
more than a futile slingshot against the skies;
but we did not stir in time, we did not rise,
and somewhere perhaps the sound of faint Satanic mirth
will follow the little people and their little star
spiralling in a space they could not guess,
falling smokily afar in little curves to nothingness.

Apocalypse

After the mushroom shapes of cloud obscure
the sun and moon and stars for forty nights,
and from their little test tubes crushed to powder
men have watched eternity pour out,
and nowhere men have breathed is air to breathe,
when Leningrad is one with Nagasaki,
Hiroshima and San Francisco twins,
when Washington and Moscow lie together
mated, inseparable silhouettes of dust—
the embers of Kharkov, Chicago, Gorki, New York
scattered anonymous upon the seas
or in suspension over some smouldering plain—
God may conceivably brood a solemn moment
upon the doctrine of gradual revelation.

He may perhaps regret his methodism,
grieve the free will he gave his little man,

bemoan the sacrifice he made one Easter,
decide to try upon another planet
His Love and Skill and Hope.

                                      And when the nights
acrid with death and desolation pass
into the only Memory surviving,
the light of sun and moon and stars may show
one little pile of rocks upon the crust
of what was once the crawling earth where suddenly
some movement stirs the poisoned ash, disturbs
earth's final, irremediable quiet . . .

                                    A shape
naked and bleeding may grope on hands and knees
to twist and grasp its way toward the pile's black top,
and there with vacant eye and seeming random movement

bind by flaking wire one long charred stick
across another stick and place this sign
upright between two stones. And then fall dead.

A fitting act, for there should be some token
to mark the passing of a race, to leave
the dying earth some kind of monument.

Ultimate Weapon

Having dared for long the ambivalent arrows,
the outrageous slings, man is not likely now
to flutter away like the city's neurotic sparrows
because his electronic monsters throw
their mushroom heads against prophetic skies.

Terror makes not darkling fires in his eyes.

He considers casually the wonder he has wrought
like Buddha contemplating his usual navel,
remembers the price for which the blast was bought,
and calculates its worth in open trade.

He wields oblivion the way he wields a gavel.

This is the way the proud invincible are made.

You will not frighten man or make him slave
with blueprint threat or test-tube spell or pain,
with fission nuclear, infinitive,
or trichological.

                                        One weapon, thin,
subtle as hair, alone may press him back
into the jungle he prowled when he was young—
the Devil's clever tool, the forked tongue.

This way only lies the sure attack.

Nothing that walks or swims or flies or lurks
beneath a microscope, nothing that leaps
off the farthest rim of the astronomer's adventurous glass,

has daunted man, has stayed his earnest works
for God and self (but mostly self). He sleeps
in a windswept place where wonders come to pass
and wakes to make them real.

                                      Man lives undaunted
but prey to one insidious assault
that probes the tight defenses he has vaunted,
that pounds his mind's soft underbelly, the ear.

Out of the air to force his impregnable vault
streaks the secret weapon of doom and fear,
and man who was invincible has heard
the boldly lying but the credible word.

The Edge of Oblivion

i FINAL CURTAIN

Assuming there were celestial ticket-holders
to fill the problematic stalls and then
imagining a prestidigitator
voicing his patter and waving his aluminum tube,
making a puff of smoke . . . and Presto! Look . . .
a world where men walk double-imaged, split
within themselves the way they split the atom
and equally charged with menace.

                            The audience
might well stare unbelieving, might lean their halos
close together and whisper "Does it with mirrors."

How else explain incredibilities?

Enswarmed upon a supine continent,
bipeds acquire by edict behavior pattern
lateral in type whereby left hands are kept
insulate against all hints of action
right hands are poised to take. By martial law
the brain's geography, securely cased
between his hairy ears since man evolved,
is now revised so that an iron curtain
divides the two cerebral hemispheres.

The physiologists have long described
a fissure longitudinal that holds
these entities apart; but they have shown
that each possessed a ventricle containing
cerebrospinal fluid so that the two
might keep in touch . . . if all else failed might settle
for a kind of purposeful osmosis. But now
the fissure, ossified by legislation,
becomes first calcium, then bone, then metal.

The split becomes dichotic, too. The ears
receive a different sound from either side:
the little golden hammers from the right
that beat upon tympanum tight-stretched there
convey a sound that cannot pass the wall;
the little iron hammers from the left
strike on the left-hand drum and their noise also
can permeate one hemisphere alone.

Thus we have Man bisected from within,
marching in single file but seeing double,
having a single number but a party line,
conditioned to keep all love and hope apart,
in a designated lobe, from hate and fear
which have their own restricted lobe. But worse,
we see Man tend in half the world to turn
his hate and fear toward right-hand ganglions,
while in the other half these two fixations
begin to occupy the left-hand lobe.

"Does it with mirrors" has a certain logic,
for how else could this spectacle be worked?
A half a billion men who seem aligned
in hate and fear to half a billion men
who in their turn reveal but half their mind.
To those who might conceivably be watching
this pageantry of doom, the final scene
would seem effectively contrived. For Man,
stripped of his mind's once shining arms and armor,
holds his hands between himself and the night,
then, breathing a prayer to his half-forgotten gods
through teeth that chatter in imbecilic fright,
stretches ten digits against disintegration.

ii NOW AT THE EDGE OF OBLIVION: MEMORIES OF
HARVARD AT MIDCENTURY
(For Kenneth W. Porter, Ph. D., Harvard '36)

We walked across the yard from Eliot House
kicking at russet leaves and kicking at the pricks
of the literary fates. Our noses, the times,
the critics, and taste were out of joint. Remember
how we despaired because all songs were sung,
all reputations made? The world was done
with war and challenge and romance and even windmills;
you said a thing I thought of many times
in the years to come: "History has cut our throats
we should have come along in time to write
sonnets in trenches; or lacking that we should
have had hurt Jewish eyes or a black skin."

We had no place, we cried. Recall the year?
The Waste Land was ten years old; the Wall Street Crash,
three years behind us, was still to blame
for the ills of the world. And the world was being saved
by a curious symbol sprung in phrase from England—
a Hyde Park orator. But we in the yard
had more to think about than symbol phrases;
we had reality: Thomas Stearns was back.

And we who knew by heart the Trinity—
Babbitt and Kittredge and Lowes—were struck to note
that here we had the Three-in-One; that doubting
Thomas had spent his eighteen years in England
steeping the olden gospels, clipping the texts,
adding a spice of Corbiere, Laforgue,
and Baudelaire skimmed from Symon's Symbolist,
stirring well with parts of Bradley salvaged
from doctoral thesis never converted to symbol . . .
and now served up precisely under the aegis
of the neatly packaged Norton lecture series.

We had no further need for Kittredge, Lowes,
or Babbitt (remember you said "He kept his notes! "
and I said "Eighteen years! My God, in eighteen years
will we recall we ever went to Harvard?"
And do we, Friend? Do you, as I, spend nights
wishing this were the Yard again, the future
veiled from wildest guess, and God's Great Finger
pressed upon the calendar to make
the years stop short at 1932?).

At one deft pronouncement you snorted "Kitty's notes"
but I thought Lowes until you said "If so
it's out of Kittredge; Lowes is far too new"
and we beheld in that small calculation
the beauty of learning's dogged will to survive
through marriage with self, through laying the self's
                                    own egg!

We slept the lecture through the night. We knew
the truth so well we did not need once more
to hear it all again. We slept and dreamed.

And that was eighteen years ago this month.

Dear Brother, can you sleep? Do not your dreams
remind you that we heard a prophet speak
yet paid no heed because his scholarship
was second-hand; because his prose had stemmed
from men who taught us and men we too had read,
we did not grasp the vision that he keened
in *The Waste Land*.

And now a boy conceived that night
conceivably walks wide-eyed through the Yard
breathless to have September come, proud
of the Harvard years ahead that will be his.

Dear schoolmate, will they? Or will he find instead
the thing that doubting Thomas prophesied?
Will this poor boy who may not know another
eighteen years of life, like us (who did)
discover that this, indeed, is the way the world ends
"not with a bang but a whimper?" Correction: add,
the shape of things to come will doubtless be
a puff of smoke over "death's twilight kingdom"
having a moment the form of a delicate mushroom.

And none will record the final word that man
utters upon his Wasteland planet or sees
on some final, haphazard memorial fragment of stone:
had you thought it might perhaps be any sound
in any tongue that man has known? *Shantih?*

Or even a shorter word that some boy wrote
on a marble wall in a room in Eliot house
while he stood there writing his dreams in yellow water.

iii: THE LAST STAND

Look now upon this sunset with suspicion
though it behaves as if it had a schedule
filled with as many tomorrows as there were yesterdays;
for you must know that this enveloping red bloom
upon the soft dark margins of the earth
may never come again.

                                            Turning its back
upon the casual sun, the earth may make
a wider curve in space, may jump its orbit,
glow darkly a moment, then blow apart to form
a rain of gray atomic dust on the stars
that have not yet been born.

Of course you may
console yourself as Fujiwara did
(saying the cuckoo on the mountaintop
makes no sound with no one there to hear him)
and think it does not matter if you or earth
plummet first to nowhere. But you know it does.

Look now upon this sunset with suspicion.

* * *

Look well upon the falling leaves this year
for the skies themselves may fall another season;
study the silhouette against the sun
of objects vertical, of steeples, trees,
and chimneys round as poles. All this may soon
level itself to smudged and rubbled plains,
smouldering wrathful recollection
of days when man, engaged in saving face,
better had saved the firm and standing stone.

Look well on man himself who stands so bold
against a crimson afterglow of day,
for in his nimbus burns the neon code
which can be broken down to read in clear
astringent message of oblivion.

And Now in Search of Peace

This we have known before: the clumsy metal
caterpillar tread, the zooming wings,
the little bees of death with fatal stings,
the sudden flash, the rise with crimson petal
of ugly flowers planted by explosion.

This we have known before: the halt, the blind,
the mad, the bitter, roaming the earth to find
escape; the heartsoil knowing quick erosion.

This we have known before: the quiet years
balanced on precipice of hope; the praying
never to know again a preacher saying
"Go to the wars in Jesus' name;" the fears.

That which has been will be, but, looming bigger,
will come in shape to puzzle man's believing;
though little the change in shape of woman's grieving
if skulls be crushed by tank or olden trigger.

The death, the flight, the fear has come before
and gone before and come and gone again . . .
and now in search of peace ten million men,
hopeful, go forth another time to war.

VII. The Tired Heart: A Cardiac Biography

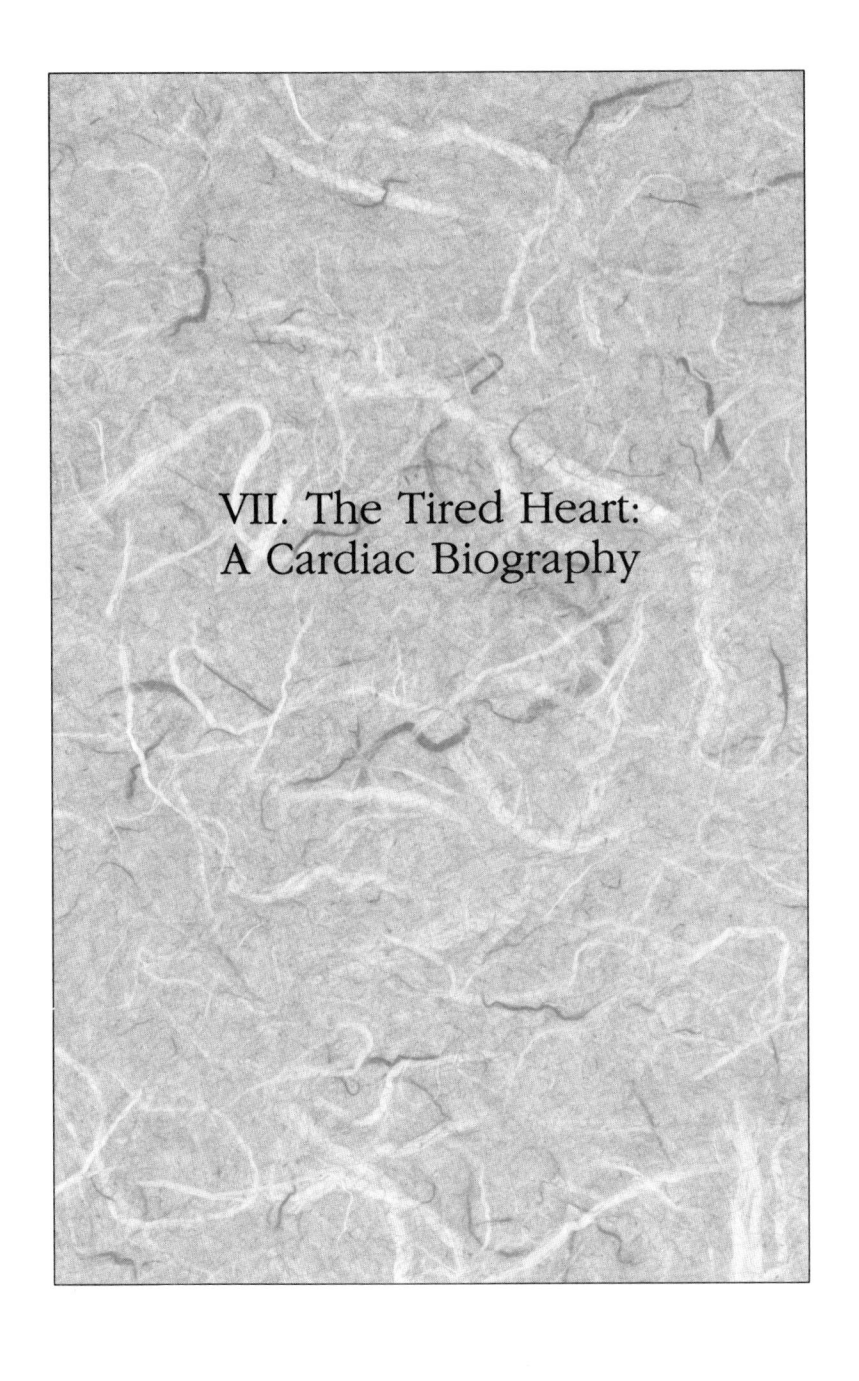

Noise of Futility

The strange deep-sounding noise of the tired heart
pulls at the ears and the throat, and blurs the eyes
of him who possesses grief; and if he start
numbly to hone the silver-clean precise
and feather edge of cutlery, he finds
the stillness about him in a way
that drains his pulse. With slow despair he grinds
under his heel the blade that was to slay
sadness forever. There is no word to call
the turning of wheels in the head that fill the night
with silent sound what time the shadows fall
of those who walk in death; nor word for the fright
that leans from the sky when the recent dead fail barely
to induce another death. Escape comes rarely.

Noblesse Oblige

The feet of the heart are weary now and slow
as an unwound clock; and each step drags behind
a little longer than the other. "Go,"
says the heart, but the feet hold back, fearing to find
themselves too soon upon some gaping brink
with footing lost. Meanwhile the mind of the heart
dwells on a time long gone. ("A ventricle think?"
you cry, amazed, "Aortas brood, apart
from neural pathways? Weird!" But who can tell
the deeps of the heart?) And the pictures there are quick
with the feel of youth while pulses almost swell
youngly the olden way. The heart is sick
from longing and dreams, and very tired, too;
but on it goes, the way a heart must do!

Would the Heart Escape?

Blindly the heart, pounding against the white
And slippery curve of bars that hold its cage
Upright days and tilted in the night
At such precarious angle, has no gauge
To measure centuries. Blindly the heart
In round confinement lifts a lever twice
And drops it once. This is the drudging part
that convicts play in the dark and damp with mice
running across their dreams. The nights become
One with the days, and time attains a blur
Of liftings twice and droppings once to numb
The body walls with sounds that grind and whir.

What if the door were opened from without?
Would the heart escape with some strange prisoner's shout?

"In the Heart's Deep Care"

The heart of the tired heart is weary more
than the heart itself. The tiny pulses wane,
the thin small streams dry up; the sun-red shore
of hope that once was stretched in surge, in vain
wrinkles to catch the semblance now of moisture;
now is the heart's bright basin parched with rust
and its hollow margins quiet as a cloister
long in ruins. No breeze disturbs the dust
that levels all. . . . But how the tired heart
would feel its arid ventricles convulse
to know a moment your quick rain, to start
the auricles once more, once more the pulse.

But all the tired heart has known of you these years
has been a desert, irrigate of tears.

Spring and the Tired Heart

The heart has been asleep since last November,
Dreaming its dreams of youth, of other springs,
Watching in retrospect a young heart clamber
The dizzy heights of love. The old heart sings
To pound once more upon the heels of youth
And tosses restless, afraid a bit to wake,
Knowing the open eye may see the truth
And trying to stay asleep for the dream's sake.

But April is a morning none may spurn
And wakes the heart that has been hibernate;
And April brings the heart a quick return
Of youth and other springs; and now the late
Exhausted heart is beating loud and fast.
What matter if the tired tissues last?

Strange Odyssey

In what queer odds and ends of far off places
The heart has been, only the heart can know,
And what the half-remembered nameless faces
That made it climb the throat and drown in the flow
Of its own insurgence. Often the heart was sick
And wished to rest, but traveled on and beat
High with its hope and loud with love and quick
With any given moment. But the stumbling feet
Of the tired heart drag to a vaguely heard
And distant dirge; the sound is carried off
While something like a broken bodied bird
Thrashes to stop remotely like a cough.

Now has the vagrant flesh been apprehended,
And now the heart's strange Odyssey is ended.

"Dead"

The strange deep-sounding noise has dropped away
leaving no echo, leaving no thing at all
except the place it used to be. The day
has also captured quiet, captured a pall
to wrap about its sunburned shoulders. Here
is emptiness and no voice lifts to ask
"Where are the hope, the joy, the love, the fear
that stretched these walls before the powdered mask
stiffened to stone?" This quiet is a drop
in the still sea where the soul of the tired heart
has gone. (Did you ever hear a clock stop
and try from far away to make it start?)

Look. He who held a stethoscope and heard
pronounces requiem in one brief word.

VIII. The Last Day

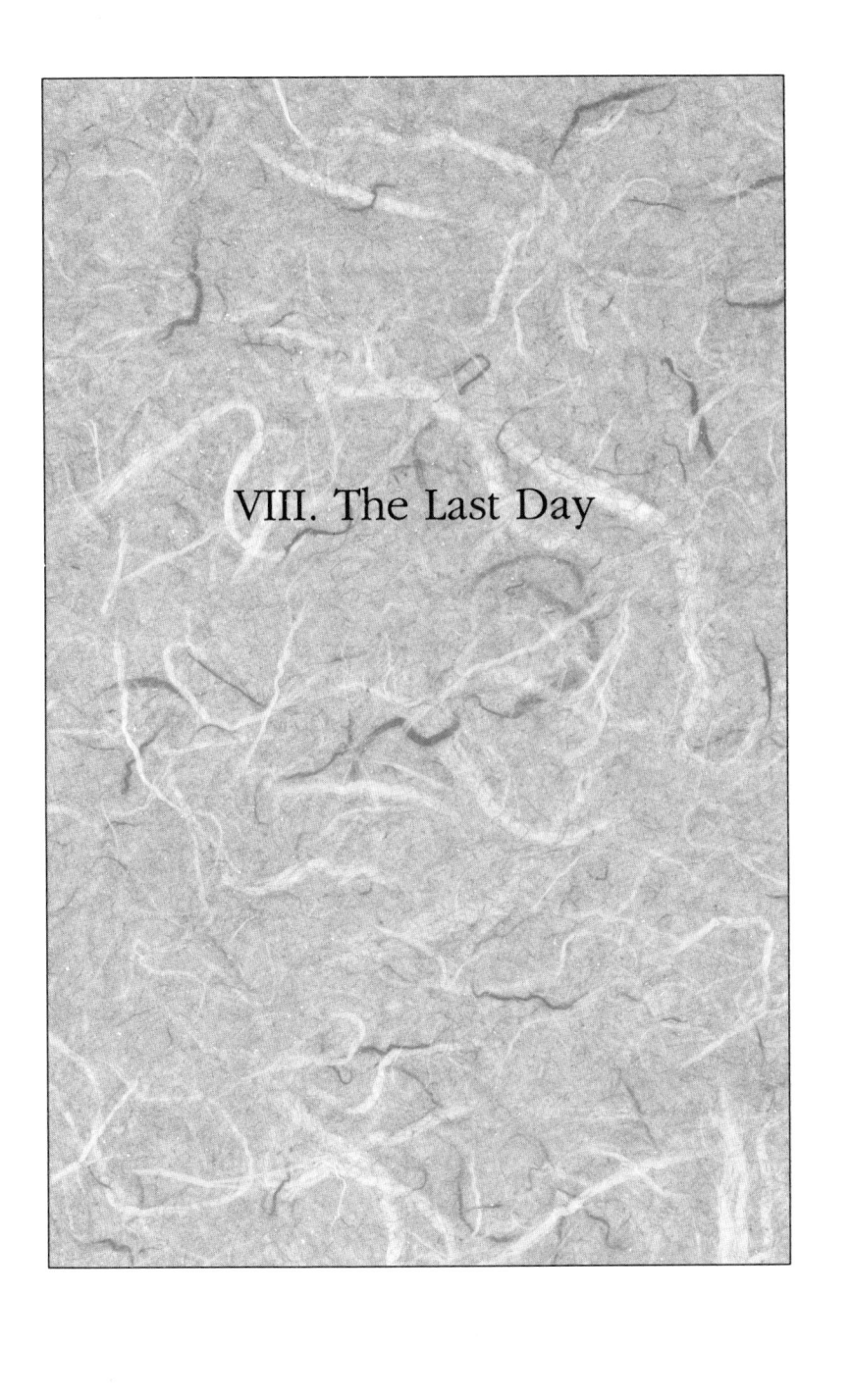

On Being Thirteen in 1970

Weep for the blind who cannot see the blue
of sky or lake or eye or paint reflecting
someone else's sight. Weep for the blind
who know a world in shadow, monochrome
with maybe flashes of darker black. Weep
long for the empty iris that never bore
the bright blossoms of sight.
                                    And weep for the
deaf, groping for some insignia of sound, some ripple
along an auditory nerve, some change
however minuscule in the hard marble landscape
of angry quiet. Weep for the deaf,
newly arrived or ancient exile here
or the native born on this bleak and silent shore.

But O weep more than this for Tommy Jones
who now thirteen with perfect eyes and ears
will spend his life, if he should live, in seeing
the blurred parabolas of small white balls,
the puff of smoke that comes when clay birds shatter,
the twirl of skirts on windy corners, the bright
hypnotic tube of glass in darkened room
that well may be the highest school he knows.

And weep for Tommy Jones who hears the loud drums
in tribal rhythm that makes his body shake,
whose ears are tuned to hear the morning clock,
the siren at noon, the whistle at five, the first
ring of a telephone that might purport
swimming or sex. Yes, weep for Tommy Jones
who will not ever see the precarious sun
balanced upon the horizon's blade, nor El Greco,
nor the slant of rain, nor the look in his father's eye;
who will not ever hear the cry of birds
(separate from the sound of shot that brings them down),
nor the wind in the trees not the thrashing surf at night

(separate from sound of fabric sliding wetly
off of four sandy legs), nor Mozart.

O weep for Tommy Jones who will not see
high in the sky the tiny mushroom cloud;
who will not hear the thunder of oblivion;
who blind and deaf in his peculiar way
will grow and mate and have a son of his own,
to look at, to hear proudly . . . in 1984.

Shelter from Oblivion

Who live in this house
       and leave in the morning, returning at night
         to eat in it, sleep in it, love and procreate in it
live on three levels:
       a top floor for sleeping, for mating, someday for dying;
       a ground floor for eating and dealing cards with friends
           and watching the *mene mene tekel*
         upon a twenty-one inch wall of lighted glass;
       and a thick-walled cellar shelter
           for crouching and waiting when the rulers remember
           to practice survival in a kind of play by Kafka . . .
live by three sounds:
       a call in the morning, a whistle at night,
       and sirens upon special unpredictable occasions–
           a bell goes off at seven . . .
            they rise and go now (to their Father's house?);
           a whistle blows at five . . .
            they drop their tools or park their trucks
            or lock their desks;
           a siren sounds and their million kin
            unworried but impatient go
            down to their cellar caves knowing that any minute
            (except the moment of truth?) they will climb up again.
Who live in this house
       are well-equipped and needy when cage sound comes:

the bell goes off at seven . . .
they respond like Pavlov's dogs;
  their toiletries are laid out neat upon the sink
  as any surgeon's implements;
they go off armed with spectacles and pens and watches,
  a pocketful of cares to prove that they are they
  and coins that bear a date no one ever looks at
    (they do not think the present year may be
    the last that man will see upon his coinage)
  and neatly furled umbrellas in the event
  that only rain will rain upon them;
the whistle blows at five
  and all the world explodes
  because all is well prepared for sudden exodus;
    out of the stone hives, bees by the million,
    out of the stone hills, ants by the million,
    up from the tunneled earth, moles by the million,
    down from the skies a myriad of walking birds;
the siren sounds the now accustomed interruption
  in single file at tempered pace
  they descend (into hell?);
  they fear only the enemy, *ennui*,
  so they are well prepared:
    mother is ready to meet her maker
    with rhythmic knitting needles;
    daughter bears cross-word puzzles
    and resupply of chewing gum;
    son is bent beneath the load
    and sodapop;
    father has a half a pint of bourbon
    and neatly folded evening paper
    which tells the day's events just past.

Who live in this house
  descend the stairs,
    look blankly into space,
      think nothing of this day
        which will (someday) be their last.

Martial Concert
For a Dubious Peace

The gods of war composed this piece for brass,
For anvil chorus, bass, and tympani;
Here is the ultimate and loudest symphony
The ears of man have known. The moments pass,
Each laden, sodden, big with pressing noise,
Weaving a terrible cloth of sound with blast
For warp, and woof of shriek that cannot last
But does; making our bold unruly boys
Seem to shout and scream with mouths unheard
Like film from which the sound effects are cut;
And all the regular motifs, the rut
In which our normal harmonies are blurred,
Compete with quiet. No little sound can stir
When giants tread the keyboards of the earth.

The gods of war have given dreadful birth
To the final composition man will hear;
Proscenium eight thousand miles across
Is shaken by crescendo from the pit
And out through space man's little ears are split,
His tightened nerves benumb him to his loss.

And suddenly all sound is done. And Peace
Comes with a burst of stillness only the deaf
Can stand, or the dead. Now, Postlude in Bass Clef,
But no stir, no coughs, as horns and trumpets cease,
No rush to catch the train when clashing cymbal
And diatonic thunder die away;

Those who remain alive are numb and stay,
Watching like endless tiers of ghosts the nimble
Baton of the shrewd conductor, sleek, aloof,
As it drops unheard against his cloven hoof.

The Last Day

At nine o'clock I close my office door,
remove my hat and coat, perform the various
trifling acts of ritual that desks are for,
then, perched upon the squeaking, sharp, precarious
edge of swivel chair and thought and hope,
of fear and maybe of oblivion even . . .
I pause, suspended in space and try to cope
with time in eight impending packets riven
halfway by hungry noon

                    And while I teeter,
one of the packets wired for sound pulsates
at the telephone's quick clarion, as if a meter
were ticking off its contents. The garbled sound equates
to ear and brain an act that must be pressed
into the postmeridian unit squeezing
an act packed prior out of the fold and—lest
it be lost to history entire—pulling and teasing
seven timebomb frames of reference lumpen.

Someone plants a head with no trunk showing
between the door and frame; it moves its dumpen
timeless mouth for endless time, not going . . .
and seven symbols must do the work of eight.

Shapeless the packets now with the load divided;
like seven flatcars spilling over freight
because they carry shares of what was sided.

A forward tilt of chair and my head curves down
for a moment only posturing despair,
doubled by conscience counting off the brown
bitter tasting ticks of time. Aware
of movement then I note with kindling glance
torso with no head upon it bent before
a filing drawer. Not mine the file or dance

of silken rump, but mine the eager store
locked in the past now fondled once again.

Away fond rumpen past. What's needed here
is stretching, a yawn, and movement with other men
to coffee bars. Then back with will . . . but fear
strangles hope by counting one to six.

The head that was buried in files now floats too close
remindful of all that holds it up; my tongue licks
parched lips; the head's mouth opens to utter "Boss."

So I arise and go to my Father's place . . .
with no resentment now of time's escaping;
all time is His who orders all my days,
Him do I serve when sitting, bowing, scraping;
and having helped Him pick a Christmas gift
for His Wife and Her Mother, once more can borrow,
poised upon the edge of time to shift
ticking packets, space from later and tomorrow.

And gaily rise to face the growling noon.
At one o'clock I close my office door,
lean back upon my chair and brood how soon
the meeting is . . . and fear counts one to four.

One word I say before the meeting closes
and say it twice. "Well," I repeat. Two wells.
Behind me half a dozen eggs with noses
stare at my neck through narrow cracks in the shells
watching me go to vanquish time once more.

My index finger quite apart from will
plays by remote control a clockwise score
to let me hear a friendly voice. The mill
of a minor god grinds small and stops for tea;
tension relaxes; two friends escape the strain
staring in space and liking what they see.

Before I dare to face my desk again
I must be groomed and otherwise prepared;
cascades of water flush my fears away,
sound in my ears as, wishing that I dared
escape, I face the chores that turn me gray.

"Miss Roberts, take a letter, please: Dear Lord
what comes of time! No, cross that out, my dear."

I try to think. One hour. With one accord
two glances travel clockward. One drops near
noting (the hundredth time?) how oftentimes
stupid girls have thought-provoking thighs . . .

"Dear Sir: We note your Atom Ads have rimes
stressing defense precautions; this belies
the dignity of warning. We feel that prose
carries the message better. Sincerely yours . . ."

Squeaking, the chair leans back. Miss Roberts goes
to groom herself for homeward battle. The force
of habit places the undone acts in piles
waiting tomorrow and maybe. Vagrant thought:
what if tomorrow . . .? Nonsense; lock the files . . .
secure the paper wonders man was wrought.

At five o'clock I shut my office door;
the word Defense on the dark glass suddenly splinters;
somewhere sirens clamor, shoutings pour
coldly down my spine; a million winters
bleach my eyes; as if in piled-up spite
all time explodes. I pull away and plummet
down into space, down into the last blanched night
with hall and wall beneath my feet and grommet
sprung from army cap above my head . . .
perhaps the only halo I shall wear
for somehow I do not feel like the honored dead
nor somehow in time's last fraction do I care.

The Last Burlesque Show

They paid their silver money and took their choice
which was to sit there still and watch the turns
blurring before their eyes so fast the voice
of every actor sounded garbled. Burns
on the gilt proscenium unheeded,
smoke backstage ignored, the show goes on:
the troupers prance, grimace, with foreheads beaded,
the straight man spiels, the stooge is put upon;
the seventh veil is lifted, G-strings hog
the moment musical. The curtain falls
on breathless climax hazed in purple fog;
the little people, wide-eyed, dumb in their stalls,
suddenly stricken, not unpleasantly, blind,
watch the world black out with a bump and a grind.

Singing Mother

You did not linger with us long,
    You could but stay a day.
You made a poem and sang a song
    And then you went away.

You were not made of our clay,
    To tread our common sod.
We might have known you could not stay,
    Ambassador of God!

Concrete Rhapsody in Georgia
(For Poet-Professors Jerry Hall and Nancy Gavrikis and Poet-Editor Mary Bolgert, Co-Founders of the Neo-Concrete Movement . . . to cement our relationships)

P's all over
    we PRODUCE
        Peaches
            Pines
                Peanuts
                    Pecans
Peaches are MADE to be probed
Pines are PULPED for PAPER to carry PresiDENTIAL PROCLAMA-
TIONS

Peanuts take PRIDE in putting people in to the COMIC SYN
        DICATES and the WHITE House
            GET YOUR PICTURE
                TOOK WITH BILLY in Plains;
            SEE THE PLACE where Amy
                TOOK HER STAND

Pecans are SET
    in MO
            lases to
                become PRESS PIES
    and PRA
            LINES are better
                when made with
                    Georgia
                        NUTS!

SO you AGRO
        NOMISTS
            Mind
                your
                    PEAS
                      and
                          Cues!

P.S.
>   YANKEES
>   GO
>   HOME.

                    Gord
                        den
                            LI
                                NK

A Prayer for John McEnroe Before Wimbledon

Father, forgive me for the sin
    of letting myself want to pray
    for the outcome of a sporting event—
I shall seek penance for being
    tempted to hope that the shoulder
    of John McEnroe would give out
    or that he would slip and sprain his ankle.

Meanwhile, I pray that no harm
    should come to him.
Protect him, Father, from the sins
    of conceit and arrogance
    that would fill his soul
    should he win this match.

Prayer for a Second Planting

We bend a second time to plant a tree;
we say we place it here to be a sign
of trees to come, of lifting trees to line
the paths across a terraced tract.

And what we mean is—here we take our stand:
here where we perform this simple act
we too will grow and spread,

learning will grow and spread,
after the trees and all of us are dead.

Nature demands a pairing as Noah knew,
so here we pause to add a second tree
almost too late
to mate
the early one.
But now that we are done,
let there be mating among the trees,
let there be abandonment of pods
and seeds and thistles.

Where these trees stand, let the thick woods grow
with clean-limned paths that men cut through—
let them, growing, be symbol, too,
as was intended.

Let the seeds and pods and thistles of thinking
leap the slopes like green and russet fire,
cover the Wasteland of the mind with verdured seas
anchored to these two stripling yoeman trees.

Let there be geometric progression
of pods and seeds and thistles,
small petals of explosion in minds and trees,
let there be multiplication of trees and minds,
let there be infinity of trees and minds,
let there be campus here. Amen.

Anne Arundel Community College
May 23, 1965

A Balladelle of Foxhunting

The master of hounds has lifted his cap;
He holds in leash the little thunder
Of myriad dripping mouths; the snap
That eager dog-jaws make in wonder
At man's unhaste and sloth and blunder
Bulges my own tight jawbone round,
And I stretch my ears for the starting cry.
Tallyho! We're off! And off, each hound.
The fox breaks cover, skims the ground,
Holding his brush against the sky.

My mount has beaten the horn; my slap
Upon his flank was never needed.
We jump a fence and leap a gap
Before the echoes have receded
From the blatant call. And all unheeded

Are the things that cross our blurring road
Or things that grow or things that fly;
The saddle bears exalted load . . .
Only the fox exists for goad,
Holding his brush against the sky.

Yoicks! Oh Yoicks! The hounds have spanned
The little space; no use to try
Muting my shouts the while I stand
Over the prize with palsied hand,
Holding his brush against the sky!

The Singing Men
(For Padraic Colum)

i

What can it be that makes them as they are,
the singing men who rise from singing soil,
who grow compact of laughter, love, and toil,
of hate and tears; of hate for Cononobar
and tears for Deidre; hate for any scar
twisting the face of freedom, tears that boil
for any body's hurt; and laughter to coil
about the hills and leap from star to star,
of love for home that bends the highest places
low to the step and makes the toil a joy
if bones be wracked in Erin's name; or faces
shining and voices raised and every boy
sudden a man with heart and loin stretched tight
because a spot of green has crossed his sight.

ii

It must be this that makes them so. The green
of ancient hills pressed smooth by centuries
must rest their souls and tamp a subtle frieze
of myriad warrior sounds against the clean
walls of their thinking. The shade they wear to keen
their tribal dead, to wrap their memories,
must work its own mysterious chemistries
to leave a temper catalytic, lean;
there must be secret strength in Irish tales,
told by an Irish nurse, and frightened winds
plucking at cottage sills; but each one nails
from long ago and far in the world's green ends;
and when these singers cry their sad desire,
their slow notes march clean-limned in strange green fire!

Esoteric Question

The poet had the key to what he said
and having said it threw the key away,
leaving the door locked tight against my hand,
shut firm against my shoulder, boot or knee.

But time has helped me disregard all doors
and I no longer hope that they will yield
to any keyless vagrant. A bird soars;
what matter if it drop to cage or field?

The poet is now in far worse straits than I
for he has spent his years in angry scorn
of those who dream but know not how or why . . .
beating his breast for ever being born.

Books on the stupid people line his shelf,
but who will explain the poet to himself?